burgoo

b u r

Justin Joyce & Stephan MacIntyre

goo

FOOD FOR COMFORT

FIGURE 1 PUBLISHING *Vancouver*

Cataloguing data available from Library and Archives Canada
ISBN 978-0-9918588-4-2

Cover and interior design by Peter Cocking
Cover and interior photography by Robert Shaer
Printed and bound in Canada by Friesens
Distributed in the United States by Publishers Group West

Figure 1 Publishing
Vancouver BC Canada
www.figure1pub.com

Contents

. . . .

Introduction

·······························

IRST AND foremost, welcome to the Burgoo Bistro cookbook.
We apologize for taking so long to compile our favourite and
most popular recipes, but we trust you'll forgive us once you
dive into this easy-to-use guide. From the very beginning it has been
the Burgoo Bistro mission to provide comfort and enjoyment to all
our guests, and this book is no different. We hope you will find it a
pleasure to use and, most of all, that it will deliver delicious results to
share with your family, plus a couple of friends and neighbours.

STEPHAN · MICHAEL · KEN · JUSTIN

A Taste of History

....

WE SUSPECT you're wondering where the idea for Burgoo came from. The original concept was developed by one of our owners, Justin Joyce, who had previously operated other successful restaurants here in Vancouver. One of those restaurants offered Jambalaya and Farmer's Gumbo, a roux based chicken and prawn dish served over rice. The popularity of those two dishes prompted him to ask, what if we only served stews?

For a year or so, the idea percolated, until on a trip through the Mayan Riviera, Justin and his wife, Sara, developed a more detailed menu that they literally scribbled on a paper napkin. Now, stew covers many styles of food preparation, most cultures and their cooking practices, and at that point the plan had grown to include offerings such as casseroles and fondues—essentially any one-pot meal that could be served in a bowl. Further, the bistro had been given a working name: StewArts, as in the art of making stew.

With this barely legible—yet comprehensive—business plan tucked into his pocket, Justin was ready to pitch the idea. He approached two good friends, Stephan MacIntyre and Ken Carty, whom he'd met while playing Ultimate Frisbee. They loved the concept, and a partnership was born.

With the team in place, the menu began to take real shape. We were intentionally moving away from fussy, vertically plated dishes that were the trend in the late 1990s toward simple, healthy and comforting foods. We embraced the idea that the humble one-pot meal is food that generations of families from all over the world have relied upon. Sharing food with family and friends has always been about comforting those you care for, and this idea seemed much more important to us than jumping aboard the latest food craze. We believed that the one-pot meal epitomized comfort food, and with that in mind we broadened our offerings to include soups. At our first location, our menu was simple: bowl foods only, served in two sizes—big and kettle. Even our salads were served in bowls.

With our menu clearly in mind, we wanted to ensure that our simple, healthy and comforting food was complemented with friendly, service oriented staff and a warm, inviting atmosphere. This focus helped us realize that the name StewArts sounded too much about the food and not enough about our underlying philosophy of comfort. When we came across the word "burgoo"—that hearty flavourful stew—and discovered that it also means the picnic or gathering at which the dish is served, we knew we had the right name for our bistro. And it didn't hurt that it's a conversation starter, since most people in Vancouver have no idea what the word means. (In fact, when people hear or read the bistro name for the first time, they assume we serve burgers. We don't.) Shortly after we agreed on the name, we added the tagline *"food for comfort"* to convey the idea of the whole experience being about familiarity and comfort.

On the morning of December 27, 2001, we opened the doors of the original Burgoo Bistro on West 10th Avenue. Stephan was in the kitchen; Ken and Justin were ready in the dining room. There was no grand opening (a common practice we continue to avoid), no opening announcement, nothing. We simply wanted to get our feet under us, open the doors and hope for the best. It was a disaster, in the best way possible. Many more people than expected came through our doors: large parties, couples, families—seemingly everyone from the neighbourhood dropped by to show their support. It was the holiday season, and people were off work, visiting family, shopping and eating at our bistro. We were thankful, exhilarated and frankly overwhelmed. It had been just six weeks since we broke ground to build the bistro, and we had worked day and night to get it ready before we ran out of money.

BURGOO [ber-GOO]

Also called Kentucky Burgoo, this thick stew is full of meats and vegetables. Early renditions were often made with small game such as rabbit and squirrel. Burgoo is popular for large gatherings in America's southern states. Originally, the word "burgoo" was used to describe an oatmeal porridge served to English sailors as early as 1750.

With the bistro running, we were working as hard as ever but now for longer hours, from open till close, seven days a week. Thankfully, we decided to close on New Year's Day 2002 to catch our breath and ready ourselves to get right back into it—which is exactly what we did for the next two years.

Over that time we continued to refine both the menu offerings and the comfort culture that, we hope, is still present today. While many restaurants change their menus annually, we were changing ours seasonally, adding comfort food from around the world. Through this process we identified our most popular dishes, such as the Beef Bourguignon and the Decadent French Onion soup, which have been on our menu since day one. Of course, we were also able to determine our not-so-popular dishes. We like to think that these items simply did not get the attention they deserve the first time around, and we continue to bring them back from time to time.

The real test of a recipe's success has been your feedback. When we've strayed from the comfort path, it has been you, our customers, who have helped remind us what we do best. Thanks for sharing your feelings on our menu changes; we couldn't have improved without you. But, just so you know, we're going to keep trying to change your minds about some of those less popular menu items!

Together, we have been able to discover dishes that have become trademarks of our menu, such as the Straight Up Tomato soup and the Gooey Cheese Grillers, affectionately called the After School Special if ordered together. In all our years, we have stuck by our theme, and it has allowed us to expand our comfort offerings to starters, sandwiches and beyond. No matter what, each dish has that hallmark characteristic—the familiar homestyle feel of a Burgoo menu item. Many of these items have even become customer and staff favourites—our Burgoo classics.

GROWING COMFORT AND COMMUNITY

In 2003, Michael Carty joined our ownership group. His marketing experience allowed us to more broadly consider our business model and our decision making. His investment of time and money also enabled us to expand into our North Vancouver location, which opened in March 2006. Another location quickly followed, on Main Street in Vancouver, in June 2008. To be honest, we were wholly unprepared for the immediate acceptance that this Main Street location would receive. Similar to Burgoo West 10th, it surpassed our expectations, and we were humbled by the support. We spent the next few years streamlining our locations and the company as a whole before we opened our fourth location in Kitsilano in December 2012 (another holiday opening—oops!).

It has been a profound pleasure for us to be involved with the communities in which we operate. We have had the good fortune of getting to know the merchants, the residents and the neighbourhood at large, and we look forward to opening more neighbourhood bistros in Vancouver. If you're willing to have us as your local comfort place, please let us know.

A PEEK INSIDE OUR KITCHENS

It has taken us just about eleven years to write our story and compile a list of recipes we feel clearly reflects the essence of Burgoo Bistro. Much of the inspiration for this cookbook was drawn from your requests for recipes and your many other questions. We have often been asked how to make The Spinach Salad dressing or Hot Chocolate Chili Pot and a number of other Bistro favourites. Until now we could only offer ingredient lists without procedures or recommendations. Well, your wait is over!

Finally, we'd like to thank everyone who has asked for a recipe, a tip or an ingredient, as it's your interest that has inspired us to write this book. Please keep in mind that Burgoo is about providing comfort. Likewise, the recipes in this book should not cause you any stress, even when you're trying to impress someone. Remember, they're coming over for a free meal! They'll simply be happy to be in your company and eat a good home cooked meal. Take a deep breath, have a glass of wine or a cup of tea, and dive into this book. Enjoy!

Starters & Shares

....

S TARTERS WERE a late addition to our menu. It seems funny
to think of it now, but our original menu featured just soups,
salads and stews. We soon realized that a little bit of food to
nibble on before the main course arrives can go a long way to making
people feel at ease and more comfortable. With that in mind we introduced a few small plates and shared appetizers. Two of the gems we
discovered were our Hummus and Guacamole; we also found one
item that has never been replaced or removed from our menu: the
Fonduemental, a Burgoo classic to be sure.

Further to our delight, the recipes that you're about to make have
become Bistro light fare favourites. Many of these little plates are
simple to prepare and can be made ahead of time; you may even want
to make a little extra for yourself to enjoy, as leftovers will keep well
for a couple of days.

Ceviche

·······

*lime marinated shrimp with tomatoes,
red onions and cilantro*

SERVES 4 TO 6

INGREDIENTS
·····························

½ lb cooked, hand peeled shrimp

·····························

3 to 4 ripe garden tomatoes,
seeded and diced

·····························

1 medium red onion, chopped

·····························

2 garlic cloves, minced

·····························

1 jalapeño pepper,
seeded and minced

·····························

juice of 5 to 6 limes

·····························

½ bunch fresh cilantro, chopped

·····························

sea salt

··········

cilantro leaves and 1 lime,
in wedges, for garnish

·····························

MARINATED FISH and seafood dishes are found all over
Central and South America, but our version of ceviche
is the familiar one from Mexico made with lots of lime and
cilantro. True ceviche is "cooked" with the acid from the lime
juice, so if you plan to make a traditional raw ceviche, use
only the freshest seafood, slice it very thinly and marinate
it in 1 cup of lime juice (juice of 6 limes) for at least 1 hour,
refrigerated.

In this recipe we use sweet, cooked and hand-peeled
shrimp, which essentially makes it a quick and easy fresh
seafood salad. Ceviche should be eaten right away after marinating. Serve with corn tortilla chips, or boiled potatoes,
grilled corn on the cob, sliced avocados, fresh lettuce leaves ...
use your imagination!

IN A LARGE BOWL, toss shrimp, tomatoes, onions, garlic,
jalapeño, lime juice, cilantro and a pinch of sea salt. Cover
with plastic wrap and refrigerate for at least 1 hour to marinate. Transfer ceviche to a glass serving bowl, and garnish
with cilantro leaves and some extra lime wedges on the side.

Guacamole

....

mashed fresh avocados with lime, jalapeños,
red onions and cilantro

SERVES 4 TO 6

FRESH AND healthy, guacamole is the perfect summer-time scooper with organic yellow corn tortilla chips and cold *cervezas*. It is great as a party dip, and we have been known to spread it on sandwiches at Burgoo, where it can make a classic BLT over the top delicious.

CUT AVOCADOS IN half lengthwise, remove and discard the pit, and scoop the flesh into a large bowl. Mash avocado until smooth but still slightly chunky—rough and rustic is what we're trying to achieve.

Stir in onions, jalapeño, cilantro, garlic, lime juice and cumin until well combined. Season to taste with sea salt, freshly ground black pepper and more lime juice. Scoop guacamole into a large, wide bowl and garnish with cilantro leaves.

INGREDIENTS

....

5 to 6 ripe, soft avocados

....

1 medium red onion, chopped

....

1 jalapeño pepper,
seeded and minced

....

½ bunch cilantro, chopped

....

1 to 2 garlic cloves, chopped

....

juice of 2 to 3 limes

....

pinch of ground cumin

....

sea salt and freshly
ground black pepper

....

cilantro leaves for garnish

....

Hummus

....

*a garlicky chickpea and tahini purée
from the Middle East*

SERVES 4 TO 6

INGREDIENTS

2 cans (each 19 oz) chickpeas,
drained and rinsed

½ cup tahini

juice of 2 lemons

5 to 6 garlic cloves, peeled

pinch of ground coriander

pinch of ground cumin

¼ cup extra virgin olive oil

½ cup water (or more)

sea salt and freshly
ground black pepper

extra virgin olive oil,
chopped fresh parsley and
paprika for garnish

WE CERTAINLY don't shy away from using a lot of garlic in our version of hummus. This healthy, versatile spread or dip should be considered a staple of your fridge or party platter and can be transformed into many delicious variations with the addition of caramelized onions, roasted peppers or sundried tomatoes, fresh basil or cilantro, or any combination of the above. Serve with warmed pita or any flatbread or with fresh cut vegetables for dipping.

USING A FOOD processor or a hand blender, roughly purée chickpeas, tahini, lemon juice, garlic, coriander, cumin and olive oil. With the motor running, slowly add water to form a very smooth paste. Season to taste with sea salt and freshly ground black pepper.

Spoon hummus onto a large, wide bowl or a plate, drizzle very lightly with olive oil and garnish with parsley and paprika.

Old Country Dip

a rustic white bean, chard, garlic and
parmesan dip with fresh herbs

SERVES 4 TO 6

THIS LOVELY, fresh-tasting dip instantly conjures up imagery of a late summer picnic in the Tuscan country-side. Crusty bread, sliced prosciutto, fresh vegetables and a crisp, clean white wine would complete this experience and cost less than a flight to Italy! This dip is also delicious, in place of rice or potatoes, served under seared fish or roasted lamb. Use cannellini beans (Italian white beans) or substitute white kidney or navy beans.

IN A LARGE, wide pot, heat some olive oil on medium-high. Add onions, chard and garlic and sauté lightly until slightly golden, 3 to 4 minutes. Add beans, water, lemon juice, a little sea salt and freshly ground black pepper and reduce the heat to a simmer. Cook for about 5 minutes, stirring vigorously once in a while to break up some of the beans. Use the back of a spoon to mash the beans against the side of the pot, but leave some beans whole, as this dip is rustic and chunky. When most of the liquid is reduced and thickened, remove the pot from the heat and stir in rosemary, parmesan and parsley. Season to taste with more salt and freshly ground black pepper.

Scoop warm dip into a serving bowl, drizzle with olive oil and garnish with parsley.

INGREDIENTS

extra virgin olive oil

2 medium white onions, diced

½ bunch red or green chard, chopped

6 to 8 garlic cloves, chopped

2 cans (each 19 oz) cannellini beans, drained and rinsed

½ cup water

juice of 1 lemon

sea salt and freshly ground black pepper

2 sprigs fresh rosemary, stems discarded and leaves chopped

½ cup shredded fresh parmesan cheese

½ bunch fresh italian parsley, chopped

extra virgin olive oil and sprigs of fresh parsley for garnish

Fonduemental

....

our take on molten gruyère and emmenthal fondue

SERVES 6 TO 8 PEOPLE FONDUE STYLE

INGREDIENTS

1 bottle (750 mL) of your favourite dry white wine

½ medium white onion, minced

2 to 3 garlic cloves, minced

½ cup whipping cream

¼ lb cream cheese, in small cubes

sea salt and freshly ground black pepper

splash of kirsch to taste (1 to 2 tbsp)

3 tbsp cornstarch

1 cup grated gruyère cheese

1 cup grated emmenthal cheese

1 cup grated mozzarella cheese

1 loaf crusty french bread or baguette, in 1-inch cubes

FONDUE, WHICH originated in Switzerland and France, essentially began with a very simple recipe: melt cheese in wine, then dip bread into the hot mixture. Cornstarch was later introduced to stabilize the mixture, and then, with the addition of kirsch, the popular version of Swiss fondue came into existence.

Our basic version has a few more stabilizing and flavouring ingredients than the official Swiss fondue recipe, giving it some versatility in our kitchen. To serve this fondue in the traditional way, you will need a craquelin (the pot), a fondue burner and long two-pronged forks. In addition to or instead of dipping bread into the fondue, try using fruit (grapes are good) or fresh vegetables.

IN A MEDIUM SAUCEPAN, combine ¾ bottle of white wine, onions, garlic, whipping cream and cream cheese on medium heat. Season to taste with sea salt and freshly ground black pepper. Simmer for about 10 minutes, stirring occasionally, until cream cheese melts and garlic and onions have released their flavours.

In a small bowl, briefly whisk together the remaining white wine, kirsch and cornstarch. Whisking constantly, slowly drizzle this mixture into the simmering pot. The wine and cheese base should thicken immediately as you whisk. Reduce the heat to the lowest setting and simmer for 6 to 8 minutes more, stirring occasionally, until smooth and bubbling.

Combine gruyère, emmenthal and mozzarella in a small bowl. Adding a handful at a time, stir grated cheeses into the hot wine mixture until everything combines and becomes lovely and stringy. Transfer the mixture to a fondue pot. Place the fondue pot on its base and set it over a low flame (it should be just enough to keep the mixture warm). Position the fondue in the centre of the table with bowls of bread chunks and any other dippers scattered around, so that everyone can help themselves.

Brie Fondue

·················

a variation on the traditional fondue,
made with roasted garlic, honey and brie cheese

SERVES 6 TO 8 PEOPLE FONDUE STYLE

INGREDIENTS

1 head of garlic, unpeeled

extra virgin olive oil

1 bottle (750 mL) of your
favourite dry white wine

½ cup apple juice

1 tbsp honey

½ cup whipping cream

¼ lb cream cheese,
in small cubes

sea salt and freshly
ground black pepper

3 tbsp cornstarch

2 cups diced soft brie cheese

1 cup grated mozzarella cheese

1 loaf crusty french bread or
baguette, in 1-inch cubes

THIS SWEET and creamy version of our Fonduemental (page 18) has become a mainstay on the menu and essentially captures the flavour of a wheel of brie baked with roasted garlic. We think it works quite nicely in a fondue format. Chunks of fruit (apples are good), fresh vegetables or even baked ham make delicious dippers along with the crusty bread.

PREHEAT THE OVEN to 350°F. Place garlic on a square of aluminum foil, drizzle with a little olive oil and toss until well coated. Tightly wrap the garlic in the foil and bake for 12 to 15 minutes. (The garlic should be golden brown and soft when squeezed.) Cut off the root end of the garlic, squeeze the soft flesh into a bowl and discard the skins. Mash garlic finely.

In a medium saucepan, combine roasted garlic, ¾ bottle of white wine, apple juice, honey, whipping cream and cream cheese on medium heat. Season to taste with sea salt and freshly ground black pepper. Simmer for about 10 minutes, stirring occasionally, until cream cheese melts.

In a small bowl, briefly whisk together the remaining white wine and cornstarch. Whisking constantly, slowly drizzle this mixture into the simmering pot. The wine and cheese base should thicken immediately as you whisk. Reduce the heat to the lowest setting and simmer for 6 to 8 minutes more, stirring occasionally, until smooth and bubbling.

Combine brie and mozzarella in a small bowl. Adding a handful at a time, stir cheeses into the hot wine mixture until everything combines. (The rind from the brie is delicious but may not melt; if you want a smooth fondue, press the mixture through a fine mesh strainer.) Transfer the mixture to a fondue pot. Serve with bowls of bread chunks as per the Fonduemental.

Queso Fuego

....

*a Mexican cheese fondue made spicy
with chorizo and chipotle*

SERVES 6 TO 8 PEOPLE FONDUE STYLE

L ET THE *fundido* begin … When we first put this dish on
our menu, we listed it as Queso Fundido, a version of
fondue found in Mexico in which cheese is melted and served
with other ingredients arranged on top. (When the cheese is
flambéed at the table for show—preferably with tequila!—
it becomes Queso Flameado.) This recipe became a favourite
of staff and guests alike, especially for that playful one-liner.

Now known affectionately as just Queso, our version
follows our usual fondue style, while incorporating many of
the traditional flavours of Queso Fundido with some *fuego*
(fire) from the chipotle. Although we use mozzarella in this
recipe, traditionally oaxaca cheese is used for its stringiness.
This cheese and small cans of chipotle en adobo can be found
in any specialty store's Mexican section. Cherry or grape
tomatoes, alongside a big mound of tortillas, are good
dipping items for this fondue.

IN A MEDIUM SAUCEPAN, heat some olive oil on medium-
high. Add chorizo, jalapeño, onions and garlic and sauté
until slightly golden, 5 to 6 minutes. Stir in chipotle, cilantro,
oregano, lime juice, cumin and sea salt to taste and sauté
for another 2 to 3 minutes until all liquids have evaporated.
Reduce the heat to medium.

Pour in 2½ bottles beer, whipping cream and cream cheese
and simmer for 5 to 6 minutes, stirring occasionally, until
cream cheese melts.

In a small bowl, briefly whisk together the remaining beer
and cornstarch. Whisking constantly, slowly drizzle this
mixture into the simmering pot. The beer and cheese base
should thicken immediately as you whisk. Reduce the heat to
the lowest setting and simmer for 6 to 8 minutes more, stirring occasionally, until smooth and bubbling.

Adding a handful at a time, stir mozzarella (or oaxaca
cheese) into the hot beer mixture until everything combines
and becomes lovely and stringy. Transfer the mixture to a
fondue pot. Serve as per the Fonduemental, with a big bowl
of tortilla chips.

INGREDIENTS

extra virgin olive oil

1 to 2 links fresh chorizo,
casings removed

1 jalapeño pepper,
seeded and minced

½ medium red onion, minced

2 to 3 garlic cloves, minced

1 tbsp chipotle, puréed
or finely chopped

½ bunch fresh cilantro, chopped

¼ bunch fresh oregano, chopped

juice of 1 lime

½ tsp ground cumin

sea salt

3 bottles (each 330 mL)
lager beer, such as Corona

½ cup whipping cream

¼ lb cream cheese,
in small cubes

3 tbsp cornstarch

3 cups grated mozzarella
or oaxaca cheese

1 bag blue or yellow corn
tortilla chips

Stout and Cheddar Fondue

....

a hearty version of fondue,
made with Guinness and strong white cheddar

SERVES 6 TO 8 PEOPLE FONDUE STYLE

INGREDIENTS

3 bottles (each 330 mL) Guinness or any other strong stout beer

½ medium white onion, minced

2 sprigs fresh rosemary, stems discarded and leaves minced

½ cup whipping cream

¼ lb cream cheese, in small cubes

sea salt and freshly ground black pepper

3 tbsp cornstarch

2 cups grated extra old white cheddar cheese

1 cup grated mozzarella cheese

1 loaf crusty french bread or baguette, in 1-inch cubes

THIS STRONG, richly flavoured fondue appears often on our colder weather menus to provide the utmost comfort on chilly days. For a heartier flavour, try to find an extra old cheddar, aged somewhere between 1 and 5 years, depending on how sharp you like it.

Chunks of pear are great for dipping in this fondue, as are heartier breads, such as multigrain, rye or Irish soda, which complement the dark beer.

IN A MEDIUM SAUCEPAN, combine 2½ bottles Guinness, onions, rosemary, whipping cream and cream cheese on medium heat. Season to taste with sea salt and freshly ground black pepper. Simmer for about 10 minutes, stirring occasionally, until cream cheese melts and rosemary and onions have released their flavours.

In a small bowl, briefly whisk together the remaining Guinness and cornstarch. Whisking constantly, slowly drizzle this mixture into the simmering pot. The beer and cheese base should thicken immediately as you whisk. Reduce the heat to the lowest setting and simmer for 6 to 8 minutes more, stirring occasionally, until smooth and bubbling.

Combine cheddar and mozzarella in a small bowl. Adding a handful at a time, stir grated cheeses into the hot beer mixture until everything combines and becomes lovely and stringy. Transfer the mixture to a fondue pot. Serve with bowls of bread chunks as per the Fonduemental.

Mussels Espagnol

steamed mussels in a chorizo, tomato,
saffron and red wine sauce

SERVES 4 TO 6 AS A STARTER (OR 2 TO 3 AS A MAIN COURSE)

ALTHOUGH WE have only ever offered a few styles of prepared mussels on our menu, this recipe is among the longest lasting. The flavours of chorizo, saffron and red wine in this version evoke sunny Spain, so your favourite Spanish red is ideal.

HEAT OLIVE OIL in a large cast iron or enamel pot or a Dutch oven on medium-high. Add chorizo and brown, breaking up clumps of meat, for 4 to 5 minutes. Stir in onions and garlic and sauté for 1 to 2 minutes until translucent. Pour in red wine and saffron, increase the heat to high and cook until wine is almost completely reduced, 4 to 5 minutes. Add tomato paste, chicken stock, chili flakes and sea salt to taste, reduce the heat to medium and simmer for 4 to 5 minutes or until the sauce has thickened and reduced by ½. Stir in cilantro, oregano and lemon juice.

Immediately add mussels, stir briefly, then cover with a tight-fitting lid and allow the mussels to steam for 6 to 8 minutes, or until most of the mussels have opened fully. Discard any unopened mussels. Stir briefly to coat mussels with the sauce, throw some sprigs of oregano on top, garnish with lemon wedges and serve immediately.

INGREDIENTS

extra virgin olive oil

1 to 2 links fresh chorizo, casings removed

1 medium white onion, minced

4 to 5 garlic cloves, minced

⅓ bottle (250 mL) of your favourite Spanish red wine

pinch of saffron threads

2 tbsp tomato paste

1 cup good quality chicken stock

pinch of chili flakes

sea salt

½ bunch fresh cilantro, chopped

½ bunch fresh oregano, chopped

juice of 1 lemon

3 lbs fresh mussels, cleaned and debearded (tap on the shells, and if they close, they are good)

sprigs of fresh oregano and 1 lemon, in wedges, for garnish

Mussels Cocotte

*steamed mussels in a bacon, thyme
and white wine cream sauce*

SERVES 4 TO 6 AS A STARTER (OR 2 TO 3 AS A MAIN COURSE)

A BIG BOWL of mussels to share is the ultimate comfort food: the pot directly on the table, everyone digging in and serving themselves, a big plate for shells, a big crusty loaf of bread or a plate of french fries to sop up the delicious juices. Eating mussels is an event!

These mussels are often ordered as the "French mussels," but they are named for the cocotte, the large enamel pot with handles in which mussels are traditionally served. This recipe is for mariner style mussels, Moules Marinière, which are made with white wine, cream, garlic and herbs. We add bacon and a bit of Dijon mustard for extra flavour.

SET A LARGE cast iron or enamel pot or a Dutch oven on medium-high heat. Add butter and bacon and sauté until bacon is slightly crisp, 3 to 4 minutes. Stir in onions and garlic and sauté for 1 to 2 minutes until translucent. Pour in white wine, increase the heat to high and cook until wine is almost completely reduced, 4 to 5 minutes. Add whipping cream and cook for 3 to 4 minutes, or until the sauce has thickened and reduced by at least ½. Stir in parsley, thyme and mustard, and season to taste with sea salt and freshly ground black pepper.

Immediately add mussels, stir briefly, then cover with a tight-fitting lid. Reduce the heat to medium and allow the mussels to steam for 6 to 8 minutes, or until most of the mussels have opened fully. Discard any unopened mussels. Stir briefly to coat mussels with the sauce, throw some sprigs of parsley on top, and serve immediately.

INGREDIENTS

knob of butter

6 to 8 strips bacon, thinly sliced widthwise

1 medium white onion, minced

4 to 5 garlic cloves, minced

⅓ bottle (250 mL) of your favourite dry white wine

1 cup whipping cream

½ bunch fresh parsley, chopped

2 to 3 sprigs fresh thyme, leaves only, chopped

1 tbsp dijon mustard

sea salt and freshly ground black pepper

3 lbs fresh mussels, cleaned and debearded (tap on the shells and, if they close, they are good)

sprigs of fresh parsley for garnish

Soups

··

SOUPS ARE the backbone of our menu, and we have always tried to offer a wide variety, from African Peanut soup to Stephan's very own Québécois Grand Maman's Split Pea and Ham. Often customers will share their own stories of a soup their family has made for generations, and while ours may taste nothing like it, we do our best to make sure all our soups are comforting and delicious. We are always honoured that so many of you share your family food memories with us.

What's wonderful about soup is its incredible versatility. It can be sweet or savoury, brothy, creamy, smooth or chunky. It can be served warm, cold or hot, in cups, bowls or kettles and for just about any meal. It can be made with fruits, vegetables, legumes, meats, cheeses, eggs or nuts and seasoned with a seemingly endless selection of herbs and spices. So, use these recipes as a starting point and vary them according to your own tastes and food preferences. For best results, use good quality fresh stocks made with all natural ingredients and do your best to avoid the powders and cubes.

African Peanut

*a smooth and spicy curried peanut and coconut
soup finished with cilantro*

SERVES 6 TO 8

INGREDIENTS

vegetable or peanut oil

1 medium white onion, diced

2 to 3 celery stalks, diced

2-inch knob of fresh ginger,
peeled and chopped

5 to 6 garlic cloves, chopped

2 to 3 tbsp Curry Spice (page 129)

2 medium yams,
peeled and diced

1 medium ripe banana,
peeled and diced

1 can (19 oz) coconut milk

8 cups good quality
chicken stock

3 to 4 tbsp natural,
smooth peanut butter

pinch of cayenne pepper

sea salt and freshly
ground black pepper

juice and zest of 1 lime

½ bunch fresh cilantro, chopped

1 small handful chopped
roasted peanuts for garnish

THIS DELICIOUS and unusual soup is thickened with yams, peanut butter and banana. In our early years, it went over well, but, sadly, the risk of peanut allergies has made it difficult to keep on our menu.

Serve this soup in the summer with any curry or even a barbecue. For a completely vegetarian version, substitute a light vegetable stock for the chicken stock.

HEAT VEGETABLE (or peanut) oil in a large, heavy pot on medium-high. Add onions, celery, ginger, garlic and Curry Spice and sauté until onions are translucent, 3 to 4 minutes. Stir in yams, banana, coconut milk, chicken stock, peanut butter and cayenne and bring to a simmer. Season to taste with sea salt and freshly ground black pepper. Reduce the heat to low and simmer for 30 to 40 minutes, until the vegetables are very soft.

Using a blender (and working in small batches) or a hand blender, purée soup until very smooth. Return the soup to the pot and stir in lime juice, lime zest and ½ of the cilantro and simmer for 5 minutes more.

Portion the soup into bowls and garnish each with chopped peanuts and the remaining cilantro. Serve hot.

Beef Barley

·············

a rich and hearty beef broth with barley,
vegetables and a hint of rosemary

SERVES 6 TO 8

A MEAL IN a cup, beef barley is a classic hearty soup that's perfect for cold winter nights. We don't stray too far from the traditional recipes, but we like to add fresh herbs and green peas to freshen up the flavours. Barley tends to expand, soaking up all the liquid in the pot as it grows and grows, so add more beef stock if it gets away from you or if you are reheating this soup the next day.

HEAT VEGETABLE OIL in a large, heavy pot on high. Add beef, season with freshly ground black pepper and sauté, stirring occasionally, but allowing meat to brown nicely on all sides, 5 to 6 minutes. Stir in onions, celery, carrots, garlic and barley and sauté another 3 to 4 minutes until onions are translucent. Deglaze the pot with red wine, stirring and scraping to release any bits from the bottom. Add beef stock, Worcestershire sauce, tomato paste, bay leaves and thyme and bring to a boil. Season to taste with sea salt and freshly ground black pepper. Reduce the heat to low and simmer for 1 hour, until barley and beef have softened and broth has slightly thickened.

Stir in peas, rosemary and ½ of the parsley and simmer for another 5 minutes to heat through and release the flavours, then season, as necessary, with more sea salt and freshly ground black pepper. Portion the soup into bowls and garnish each serving with the remaining parsley. Serve hot.

INGREDIENTS

vegetable oil

1 lb stewing beef, in ½-inch dice

freshly ground black pepper

1 medium white onion, diced

3 to 4 celery stalks, diced

3 to 4 medium carrots, peeled and diced

3 to 4 garlic cloves, chopped

1 small handful dry pearl barley

½ bottle (375 mL) of your favourite red wine

8 cups good quality beef stock

splash of worcestershire sauce

1 tbsp tomato paste

2 to 3 bay leaves

pinch of thyme

sea salt

1 handful frozen green peas, thawed

2 to 3 sprigs fresh rosemary, stems discarded and leaves chopped

½ bunch fresh parsley, chopped

Babushka's Borscht

a hearty soup loaded with beets,
cabbage and rutabaga and served with sour cream

SERVES 6 TO 8

INGREDIENTS

3 to 4 medium red beets, diced

½ small rutabaga or turnip, diced

½ small green cabbage, diced

1 medium white onion, diced

2 to 3 celery stalks, diced

3 to 4 garlic cloves, chopped

¼ cup tomato paste

1 tbsp brown sugar

4 cups water or good quality vegetable stock

1 cup apple juice

½ bottle (375 mL) of your favourite red wine

splash of red wine vinegar

2 bay leaves

pinch of ground fennel seeds

pinch of marjoram

pinch of thyme

sea salt and freshly ground black pepper

½ bunch fresh parsley, chopped

1 cup sour cream

AT BURGOO, people let us know when we create a recipe that resembles something their mom or dad or grandma used to make for the family. Those childhood memories are powerful, and more than any other dish on our menu, our borscht sparks an emotional response. It earns many compliments—but almost as many criticisms when it doesn't taste like the one they remember.

Borscht has been adopted in so many countries in Europe, and there are so many historical family recipes, that we know we will never make the perfect borscht to satisfy everyone. The truth is, every pot of borscht is just perfect for someone, and this is our version, which is vegetarian and loved by many.

IN A LARGE, heavy pot on high heat, bring beets, rutabaga (or turnip), cabbage, onions, celery, garlic, tomato paste, brown sugar, water (or vegetable stock), apple juice, red wine, vinegar, bay leaves, fennel, marjoram and thyme to a boil. Season with generous pinches of sea salt and freshly ground black pepper. Reduce the heat to low and simmer the soup for 1 hour, or until vegetables have softened. Remove from the heat, stir in ½ of the parsley. Season to taste with more sea salt and freshly ground black pepper.

Portion the soup into bowls, dollop sour cream on each serving and garnish with the remaining parsley. Serve hot.

Butternut Squash

....

a butternut squash purée with a hint of warm spices,
maple syrup and hazelnuts

SERVES 6 TO 8

INGREDIENTS
....

1 medium-large butternut squash,
peeled, seeded and diced
....

2 to 3 medium carrots,
peeled and diced
....

1 medium white onion, diced
....

2 to 3 celery stalks, diced
....

2-inch knob of fresh ginger,
peeled and chopped
....

4 cups water
....

4 cups orange juice
....

splash of pure maple syrup
....

pinch of Winter Spice (page 131)
....

sea salt and freshly
ground black pepper
....

1 handful roasted,
roughly chopped hazelnuts
and sprigs of fresh parsley,
chopped, for garnish
....

PRETTY MUCH the perfect soup for a crisp fall day, the warm spices hint at the approaching winter months. You can substitute almost any squash, or even pumpkin, for the butternut, and this soup will work. Pair it with a nice chunk of multigrain loaf and our Winter Greens salad (page 65).

IN A LARGE, heavy pot on high heat, bring squash, carrots, onions, celery, ginger, water, orange juice, maple syrup and Winter Spice to a boil. Season with generous pinches of sea salt and freshly ground black pepper. Reduce the heat to low and simmer the soup for 1 hour, or until vegetables are soft.

Using a blender or a hand blender, purée soup until very smooth. Portion the soup into bowls, sprinkle each serving with chopped hazelnuts and parsley, and drizzle with a little maple syrup. Serve hot.

Chicken Itza

....

*a tomatillo soup with chicken and cilantro,
finished with lime, crema and tortilla*

SERVES 6 TO 8

THE NAME of this soup is a play on Chichen Itza, the famous Mayan monument on the Yucatan Peninsula in Mexico. Sometimes we like to amuse ourselves, and occasionally others, with our recipe names!

This soup is inspired by a few delicious Mexican soups— Sopa de Tomatillo, Sopa de Ajo and Sopa de Tortilla—which we decided to combine into one. Use ripe tomatillos for this recipe, letting them sit on your counter for a day or two to soften them, if need be.

IN A LARGE BOWL, toss chicken thighs with vegetable oil to coat. Season to taste with pinches of cumin and sea salt. Cover and set aside.

In a large, heavy pot on high heat, bring tomatillos, onions, garlic, jalapeño, chicken stock, 1 tsp cumin, coriander, oregano, and pinches of sea salt and freshly ground black pepper to a boil. Reduce the heat to low and simmer the soup for 1 hour.

While the soup simmers, heat a barbecue or a cast iron grill pan on medium-high. Add chicken and sear on both sides, 4 to 5 minutes per side, until nicely charred and cooked through. To test for doneness, insert a sharp knife in the thickest piece of thigh. The juices should run clear. Remove from the heat, allow to cool slightly, then roughly cut into small dice.

Remove the soup from the heat, add ½ of the cilantro, spinach, avocados, oregano and green onions. Using a blender or a hand blender, purée soup until very smooth. (Blending fresh greens into the hot soup gives it a vibrant colour and a fresh flavour.) Return the soup to the pot, place on low heat and stir in the chicken, lime juice and lime zest. Simmer for another 5 minutes to allow the flavours to blend.

To make the crema, combine equal parts sour cream and whipping cream in a small bowl.

Portion the soup into bowls, garnish with the crema, remaining cilantro, tortilla chips and a wedge of lime. Serve hot.

INGREDIENTS

8 boneless, skinless chicken thighs

vegetable oil

1 tsp ground cumin + a pinch for seasoning chicken

sea salt

12 medium tomatillos, husks removed and flesh diced

1 medium white onion, diced

3 to 4 garlic cloves, chopped

1 jalapeño pepper, seeded and chopped

8 cups good quality chicken stock

pinch of ground coriander

pinch of oregano

freshly ground black pepper

1 bunch fresh cilantro, chopped

1 handful fresh spinach leaves, chopped

2 medium avocados, peeled, pitted and roughly chopped

2 to 3 sprigs fresh oregano, chopped

½ bunch green onions, chopped

juice and zest of 1 lime + 1 lime, in wedges, for garnish

sour cream

whipping cream

2 handfuls unsalted tortilla chips

Chicken Harira

*chicken, vegetables and chickpeas
in a tomato soup with North African spices*

SERVES 6 TO 8

A TRADITIONAL BERBER soup, Harira is redolent with the warm spices found in the souks (markets) of every city in Morocco. The country's cuisine is a unique blend of influences from Europe, Africa and the Middle East, and this warm, rich soup showcases them with a healthy amount of vegetables. Once you've made this recipe, experiment with other combinations such as grilled lamb or fish instead of the chicken and whatever vegetables are in season. As long as you keep the basic spicy tomato broth, any variation will work.

IN A LARGE bowl, toss chicken thighs with olive oil, a pinch of Moroccan Spice and generous pinches of sea salt and freshly ground black pepper until well coated. Set aside, covered.

In a large, heavy pot on high heat, bring onions, celery, carrots, rutabaga (or turnip), garlic, ginger, diced tomatoes, chickpeas, tomato paste, chicken stock, orange juice, a pinch of Moroccan Spice and saffron to a boil. Season with pinches of sea salt and freshly ground black pepper. Reduce the heat to low and simmer the soup for 1 hour.

While the soup simmers, heat up the barbecue or a cast iron grill pan on medium-high. Add chicken and sear on both sides, 4 to 5 minutes per side, until nicely charred and cooked through. To test for doneness, insert a sharp knife in the thickest piece of thigh. The juices should run clear. Remove from the heat, allow to cool slightly, then roughly cut into small dice.

Add chicken, zucchini, ½ each of the parsley and mint to the soup and simmer for 5 more minutes to blend the flavours and soften the zucchini.

Portion the soup into bowls and garnish each serving with the remaining chopped herbs. Serve hot.

INGREDIENTS

8 boneless, skinless chicken thighs

extra virgin olive oil

2 pinches Moroccan Spice (page 130)

sea salt and freshly ground black pepper

1 medium red onion, diced

2 to 3 celery stalks, diced

2 medium carrots, peeled and diced

½ small rutabaga or turnip, diced

2 to 3 garlic cloves, chopped

1-inch knob of fresh ginger, peeled and chopped

1 can (19 oz) diced tomatoes with juice

1 can (19 oz) chickpeas, drained and rinsed

¼ cup tomato paste

8 cups good quality chicken stock

2 cups orange juice

pinch of saffron threads

1 small zucchini, diced

½ bunch fresh parsley, chopped

½ bunch fresh mint, chopped

Crab Bisque

·················

smooth crab and red pepper cream
bisque with tarragon

SERVES 6 TO 8

INGREDIENTS

1 medium yam, peeled and diced

1 medium white onion, diced

2 to 3 celery stalks, diced

2 cans (each 19 oz) fire roasted
red peppers, drained and diced

2 tbsp tomato paste

½ bottle (375 mL) of your
favourite white wine

4 cups good quality
seafood stock

pinch of ground fennel seeds

sea salt and freshly
ground black pepper

1 cup whipping cream

½ lb or more cooked crabmeat

½ bunch fresh tarragon, chopped

1 lemon, in wedges, for garnish

OVER THE years we've made several bisque variations, most of them with a creamy red pepper base but with different seafood and herbs. This version made with crab maintains a cherished place on our menu. If you should be so lucky, you'll one day enjoy it as it is best served: heated over a driftwood fire on a foggy Pacific Coast beach.

While traditional bisque is made by boiling the bodies and shells of whole shellfish, and though we've done that on many occasions, we've simplified the process since then. If you do want to buy fresh crabs, boil them and pick out the meat for this recipe, by all means do! And you can also use your boiling liquid in place of the seafood stock in this recipe.

IN A LARGE, heavy pot on high heat, bring yams, onions, celery, red peppers, tomato paste, white wine, seafood stock, fennel and generous pinches of sea salt and freshly ground black pepper to a boil. Reduce the heat to low and simmer the soup for 1 hour, or until vegetables are soft.

Using a blender or a hand blender, purée soup until very smooth. Stir in whipping cream, crabmeat and ½ of the tarragon.

Portion the soup into bowls and garnish each serving with the remaining tarragon and a wedge of lemon. Serve hot.

Curried Lentil

a curried lentil soup with warm Indian spices

SERVES 6 TO 8

INGREDIENTS

vegetable oil

2 medium white onions, chopped

4 to 6 garlic cloves, chopped

2-inch knob of fresh ginger, peeled and chopped

large pinch of Garam Masala (page 130)

6 to 8 curry leaves

2½ cups dried red lentils, rinsed

10 cups good quality vegetable stock

pinch of ground turmeric

sea salt and freshly ground black pepper

sprigs of fresh cilantro for garnish

DHAL IS a side dish or stew made with lentils, peas or beans and spiced from mild to hot. In India, it is a staple food. This vegan soup, a customer and staff favourite, came about while attempting to reproduce the flavours of dhal. Look for the curry leaves in specialty food stores, and buy some extra ones to freeze so that you always have them on hand.

Any leftovers will thicken in the fridge overnight, so add water if you're reheating this soup, or leave it thick and serve it as a side dish or as a dip for roti and naan breads.

HEAT VEGETABLE OIL in a large, heavy pot on medium-high, then add onions and sauté, stirring often, until golden, 5 to 6 minutes. Stir in garlic, ginger, Garam Masala and curry leaves, and sauté another 1 to 2 minutes to release the flavours. Add lentils along with the vegetable stock, turmeric, and generous pinches of sea salt and freshly ground black pepper. Reduce the heat to low and simmer, stirring occasionally, for 1 hour until lentils are soft and starting to break apart. This process will release some starches and thicken your soup as well. Stir vigorously to help it along. Season to taste with more salt and freshly ground black pepper.

Portion the soup into bowls and garnish each serving with cilantro. Serve hot.

Gazpacho

....

a chilled tomato and cucumber soup with
fresh herbs and olive oil

SERVES 6 TO 8

ESSENTIALLY TOMATO salad in a cup, this fresh-tasting soup is perfect for the hot summer months. Whatever vegetables you pull, pick, snip or dig fresh from your garden can pretty much be blended into a gazpacho! We add a little red wine, which doesn't get cooked out, so feel free to omit it if you don't want your guests to get unexpectedly tipsy.

USING A SHARP knife, seed 4 tomatoes, ½ of the cucumber and 1 red pepper. Finely dice the flesh and set aside.

Roughly chop the remaining tomatoes, cucumber and red pepper and place in a deep bowl. Add onions, garlic, a splash of olive oil, vinegar and red wine. Season with brown sugar and pinches of sea salt and freshly ground black pepper to taste, then mix to combine. Using a blender or a hand blender, purée soup until very smooth. You should have a slightly thickened, red purée. If needed, thin with a little cold water or more wine. Stir in the finely diced vegetables, oregano, and ½ of the parsley and ½ of the basil. Season to taste with more sea salt and freshly ground black pepper. If serving chilled, refrigerate overnight.

Portion the soup into bowls, drizzle each serving with olive oil and garnish with the remaining parsley and basil.

INGREDIENTS

12 to 15 ripe garden tomatoes

1 large long english cucumber

2 medium red bell peppers, seeded

1 medium red onion, diced

3 to 4 garlic cloves, chopped

extra virgin olive oil

splash of red wine vinegar or sherry vinegar

splash of your favourite red wine

pinch of brown sugar

sea salt and freshly ground black pepper

2 to 3 sprigs fresh oregano, chopped

½ bunch fresh parsley, chopped

½ bunch fresh basil, chopped

Decadent French Onion

deeply roasted onions in rich beef broth,
slowly baked with croutons and gooey cheeses

SERVES 6

FRENCH ONION soup is a perfect blend of simple ingredients that, brought together, create a decadent, soul warming dish. You will need 6 individual ovenproof soup tureens or bowls for this recipe, ideally with a narrow opening that flares out to the bowl. This shape keeps the bread and cheese floating on top of the soup as it bakes.

No matter how many times we remind guests that the handles on the soup bowls are VERY hot (the bowls have just come out of the oven), it's human nature to test just how hot they are. We've done it ourselves! So warn your guests, but have a little ice on hand (pun intended) and, maybe, work on your "I told you so" expression.

PREHEAT THE OVEN to broil or 450°F. Set 6 ovenproof soup bowls on a baking tray.

Heat olive oil in a large, heavy stockpot on high, add onions and sauté, stirring often, until translucent, about 10 minutes. Stir in garlic, reduce the heat to medium-high and sauté, stirring often, for 10 minutes or until onions and garlic are brown and caramelized and all the liquid is reduced. Pour in red wine, season with generous pinches of sea salt and freshly ground black pepper and boil until most of the liquid is reduced, about 5 minutes. Add beef stock and bring to a boil, then reduce the heat to low and simmer for 30 minutes. Divide the soup evenly among the soup bowls.

In a small bowl, combine mozzarella, emmenthal and gruyère cheeses until well mixed. Divide bread chunks among the bowls, carefully floating them on the soup to form a "raft," then evenly sprinkle each serving with the mixed cheeses. Bake for 6 to 8 minutes, or until cheese is golden and bubbly. Serve immediately.

INGREDIENTS

extra virgin olive oil

8 medium onions, red or white, thinly sliced

6 garlic cloves, chopped

½ bottle (375 mL) of your favourite red wine

sea salt and freshly ground black pepper

8 cups good quality beef stock

2 cups grated mozzarella cheese

½ cup grated emmenthal

½ cup grated gruyère cheese

6 slices rustic baguette, in 1-inch cubes

Grand Maman's Split Pea and Ham

*a French Canadian yellow split pea soup with
tender ham, maple syrup and thyme*

SERVES 6 TO 8

INGREDIENTS

1 small smoked pork
hock, about ½ lb

12 cups water

3 cups yellow split peas

1 medium white onion, diced

2 to 3 celery stalks, diced

1 to 2 medium carrots,
peeled and diced

2 to 3 garlic cloves, chopped

2 to 3 sprigs fresh thyme,
leaves only, chopped

3 to 4 bay leaves

sea salt and freshly
ground black pepper

½ bunch fresh parsley, chopped

pure maple syrup for garnish

STEPHAN IS originally from Montreal. This recipe is from his childhood and was first made by his grandma. It's a traditional soup, usually eaten after a hard day's work on the farm. Hearty best describes Québécois cuisine, and this soup is as hearty as they come.

IN A LARGE, heavy pot, combine pork hock and water, cover and simmer on low heat for at least 2 hours.

Stir in split peas, onions, celery, carrots, garlic, thyme, bay leaves and generous pinches of sea salt and freshly ground black pepper. Simmer for another hour or more, stirring occasionally to break up the peas so that they will release their starches and thicken the soup.

When the peas are soft and most of them have broken up, remove the soup from the heat. Using tongs, pull out the ham hock, pick off and roughly chop the meat and return it to the soup. Discard the bone. The soup should be thick, but add a little stock (or water) if you find it too dense, then stir in ½ of the parsley.

Portion the soup into bowls, sprinkle each serving with the remaining parsley and drizzle a little maple syrup on top. Serve hot.

Magical Mushroom

a creamy wild mushroom soup

SERVES 6 TO 8

THIS SOUP celebrates mushrooms in all their glory! A creamy puréed mushroom soup is augmented with wild mushrooms and then even more wild mushrooms that have been roasted with some complementary herbs. The result is quite delicious.

Choose whichever fresh wild mushrooms are available: morels, chanterelles, portobellos, shiitakes, oysters—to name a few—all work well in this recipe. Dried wild mushrooms are usually sold as packages of mixed varieties, and those will suffice for this recipe. Serve this soup with a little toasted garlic–parmesan bread on the side.

IN A LARGE, heavy pot, bring water, dried mushrooms, button mushrooms, onions, celery, leeks, garlic, white wine, thyme, marjoram and fennel to a simmer on medium heat. Season to taste with sea salt and freshly ground black pepper and cook for at least 1 hour, until vegetables are very soft.

While the soup simmers, preheat the oven to 400°F. In a large bowl, toss fresh wild mushrooms with olive oil, fresh thyme and rosemary to coat. Spread mushrooms evenly on a baking sheet and roast for 10 to 12 minutes, until mushrooms are golden and have intensified in flavour. Remove from the oven and set aside.

Using a blender (and working in small batches) or a hand blender, purée soup, adding whipping cream, until very smooth. Return the soup to the pot, add roasted wild mushrooms and ½ of the parsley and simmer on low heat for 10 minutes to allow flavours to blend.

Portion the soup into bowls and garnish each serving with the remaining parsley. Serve hot.

INGREDIENTS

8 cups water

1 small pkg (1 oz) dried wild mushrooms

4 large handfuls button mushrooms, roughly chopped

1 medium white onion, diced

2 to 3 celery stalks, diced

1 leek, white part only, sliced

5 to 6 garlic cloves, chopped

½ bottle (375 mL) of your favourite white wine

pinch of thyme

pinch of marjoram

pinch of ground fennel seeds

sea salt and freshly ground black pepper

4 large handfuls fresh wild mushrooms, sliced

extra virgin olive oil

2 to 3 sprigs fresh thyme, leaves only, chopped

2 to 3 sprigs fresh rosemary, stems discarded and leaves chopped

1 cup whipping cream

½ bunch fresh parsley, chopped, for garnish

Manhattan Clam

hearty tomato and surf clam chowder with
bacon, vegetables and potatoes

SERVES 6 TO 8

INGREDIENTS

2 cups water

sea salt

5 lbs fresh clams; alternatively use 2 cans (each 19 oz) surf clams with nectar

extra virgin olive oil

5 to 6 strips bacon, diced

1 medium white onion, diced

2 to 3 celery stalks, diced

2 to 3 medium carrots, peeled and diced

3 to 4 garlic cloves, chopped

2 cans (each 19 oz) diced tomatoes with juice

2 cups clamato juice

1 cup clam nectar or reduced clam cooking stock

1 medium yellow fleshed potato, diced

2 to 3 bay leaves

pinch of thyme

freshly ground black pepper

sprigs of fresh parsley, chopped, for garnish

THIS SOUP is Ken's favourite, and he lobbied hard for years to get it on the menu. It is very hearty and delicious and is a great alternative to cream based seafood soups and chowders. Try your best to get surf clams, which are very meaty and great for chowders, but any canned clams will do in a pinch.

IN A MEDIUM POT on medium-high heat, bring water and a pinch of sea salt to a boil. Add clams, cover, and steam for 4 to 5 minutes, or until clams have opened. Using a slotted spoon, transfer clams to a large bowl and allow them to cool. Discard any unopened clams. Pick the meat out of the shells, place it in a small bowl and discard the shells. Strain the cooking stock through a fine mesh strainer into a pot, then reduce it to 1 cup and reserve for the soup, if needed.

Heat olive oil in a large, heavy pot on medium. Add bacon and fry until crisp, 2 to 3 minutes, then add onions, celery, carrots and garlic and sauté until onions are translucent, 1 to 2 minutes. Drain off most of the fat, then stir in tomatoes, clamato juice, clam meat, clam nectar (or reduced cooking stock), potatoes, bay leaves and thyme and bring to a boil. Season with generous pinches of sea salt and freshly ground black pepper. Immediately reduce the heat to low and simmer for 1 hour, or until potatoes are soft. Season to taste with more sea salt and freshly ground black pepper.

Portion the soup into bowls and garnish each serving with parsley. Serve hot.

Seafood Potage

....

a smooth and creamy blend of vegetables,
bacon, shellfish, smoked salmon and fresh herbs

SERVES 6 TO 8

AT BURGOO we've offered many different versions of thick, rich seafood soups, from chowders to bisques to veloutés. This recipe combines all of them into one over the top, chock full of everything potage. Use our suggestions for fish and shellfish or ask your fishmonger what's fresh and use that instead.

IN A MEDIUM POT on high heat, bring water and a pinch of sea salt to a boil. Add prawns, scallops and fresh clams (or mussels), cover with a lid and cook for 4 to 5 minutes, or until clams (or mussels) have opened and prawns and scallops are cooked through and opaque. Using a slotted spoon, transfer the shellfish to a large plate to cool. Strain cooking liquid through a fine mesh strainer into a bowl and reserve. Remove and discard all shells, then transfer shellfish to a cutting board and roughly chop. Set aside.

In a large, heavy pot on medium heat, melt butter. Add bacon and fry until crisp, 2 to 3 minutes, then add onions, celery and garlic and sauté until onions are translucent, 1 to 2 minutes. Add flour and stir well to absorb the fat and make a smooth paste (called a roux), then slowly pour in white wine and 6 cups of the reserved seafood cooking liquid, stirring constantly to incorporate the roux. Reduce the heat to low, add whipping cream, potatoes, bay leaves, marjoram, dried thyme and pinches of sea salt and freshly ground black pepper. Simmer for 1 hour, stirring occasionally, until potage has thickened and potatoes have softened. Stir in shellfish, smoked salmon, fresh thyme, green onions, ½ of the parsley, lemon juice and lemon zest, then gently simmer for another 10 minutes to allow the flavours to combine. Season to taste with more sea salt and freshly ground black pepper.

Portion the soup into bowls and garnish each serving with the remaining parsley and a wedge of lemon. Serve hot.

INGREDIENTS

6 cups water

sea salt

16 fresh medium prawns, peeled and deveined

16 fresh medium scallops

2 lbs fresh clams or mussels

large knob of butter

3 to 4 strips bacon, in small dice

1 medium white onion, diced

2 to 3 celery stalks, diced

5 to 6 garlic cloves, chopped

¼ cup all-purpose flour

1 cup of your favourite dry white wine

1 cup whipping cream

1 medium yellow fleshed potato, diced

1 to 2 bay leaves

pinch of marjoram

pinch of thyme

freshly ground black pepper

3 to 4 oz smoked salmon, diced

1 to 2 sprigs fresh thyme, leaves only

1 to 2 green onions, chopped

½ bunch fresh parsley, chopped

juice and zest of 1 lemon + 1 lemon, in wedges, for garnish

Straight Up Tomato

a red wine simmered tomato soup with garlic,
drizzled with extra virgin olive oil

SERVES 6 TO 8

INGREDIENTS

2 cans (each 19 oz) diced
tomatoes with juice

4 cups water

½ bottle (375 mL) of
your favourite red wine

8 large, ripe garden
tomatoes, diced

2 medium red onions, diced

6 garlic cloves, chopped

¼ cup tomato paste

3 tbsp brown sugar

3 tbsp balsamic vinegar

extra virgin olive oil

sea salt and freshly
ground black pepper

THIS RECIPE is our version of good old-fashioned tomato soup. Pair it with the Gooey Cheese Grillers (page 73) to make our classic After School Special, especially when you need warmth on a rainy day. Heck, serve it with any sandwich that reminds you of when you were growing up.

IN A LARGE, heavy pot on high heat, bring canned tomatoes and their juice, water, red wine, fresh tomatoes, onions, garlic, tomato paste, brown sugar, vinegar and a splash of olive oil to a boil. Season with sea salt and freshly ground black pepper. Reduce the heat to low and simmer for 1 hour. Remove from the heat and allow to cool slightly.

Using a blender or a hand blender, purée soup until very smooth. Season to taste with more sea salt and freshly ground black pepper.

Portion the soup into bowls and drizzle each serving with a few drops of olive oil. Serve hot.

Sunset Corn and Chicken

....

a creamy corn and chicken soup spiked with
chipotle and cumin and served with crema, cilantro and lime

SERVES 6 TO 8

THIS CREAMY corn soup borrows flavours such as the spicy cumin and chipotle from the American Southwest and is best eaten in late summer when corn is at its peak. Bring this soup to a barbecue potluck on a summer evening, and you'll be sure to make new friends. Make the chipotle purée by opening a small 7 ounce can of chipotle en adobo and blending the contents until smooth. We use this condiment to add a smoky and spicy flavour to many of our dishes.

IN A LARGE BOWL, toss chicken thighs with vegetable oil and 1 tbsp of chipotle purée to coat. Season with generous pinches of cumin and sea salt. Cover and set aside.

In a large, heavy pot on high heat, bring 4 cups corn, yams, onions, garlic, chicken stock, 1 tbsp or more of chipotle purée, and pinches of ground turmeric, oregano and sea salt to a boil. Reduce the heat to low and simmer the soup for 1 hour, or until vegetables are softened.

While the soup simmers, heat a barbecue or a cast iron grill pan on medium-high. Add chicken and sear on both sides, 4 to 5 minutes per side, until nicely charred and cooked through. To test for doneness, insert a sharp knife in the thickest piece of thigh. The juices should run clear. Remove from the heat, allow to cool slightly, then roughly cut into small dice.

Using a blender or a hand blender, purée soup until very smooth. Return soup to the pot, stir in the 1 cup whipping cream, the remaining corn, the diced chicken and ½ of the cilantro and simmer on low heat for 5 minutes.

To make the crema, combine equal parts sour cream and whipping cream in a small bowl.

Portion the soup into bowls, drizzle each serving with crema, and garnish with the remaining cilantro and a wedge of lime. Serve hot.

INGREDIENTS

8 boneless, skinless chicken thighs

vegetable oil

2 tbsp chipotle purée

pinch of ground cumin

sea salt

5 cups fresh or frozen corn niblets

1 medium yam, peeled and diced

1 medium white onion, diced

6 garlic cloves, chopped

8 cups good quality chicken stock

pinch of ground turmeric

pinch of ground oregano

1 cup whipping cream + extra for crema

½ bunch fresh cilantro, chopped

sour cream

1 lime, in wedges, for garnish

Thai Curry Chicken

*a green coconut curry with chicken, oyster mushrooms,
basil, cilantro and lime leaves*

SERVES 6 TO 8

INGREDIENTS

4 medium boneless,
skinless chicken breasts

vegetable oil

¼ cup green curry paste

pinch of ground coriander

sea salt

2 medium white onions, sliced

2-inch knob of fresh ginger,
peeled and thinly sliced

3 to 4 garlic cloves, thinly sliced

2 lemon grass stalks, outer
leaves trimmed, thinly sliced

3 lime leaves (or zest of 1 lime)

2 cans (each 19 oz) coconut milk

2 cups good quality
chicken stock

1 large handful sliced
oyster mushrooms

3 to 4 baby or shanghai
bok choy, thinly sliced

pinch of palm sugar or
brown sugar

a few drops of fish sauce

½ bunch fresh
thai basil, chopped

½ bunch fresh cilantro, chopped

1 lime, in wedges, for garnish

3 to 4 thai red chilies,
sliced thinly (optional)

THIS RECIPE is our take on the spicy Thai soup Tom Kha Gai. Some ingredients such as the straw mushrooms and galangal in the traditional recipe can be hard to find, so we've simplified it with ingredients that are more commonly available. Lime leaves keep well frozen, so buy more than you need for this recipe and keep them in a tightly sealed bag in the freezer for future Thai dishes (or use some lime zest, if you can't find them). You can also substitute regular basil for Thai basil. If you want to spice up this soup, thinly slice Thai red chilies and allow your guests to add them at will to their soup.

IN A LARGE BOWL, toss chicken breasts with vegetable oil and ½ of the curry paste to coat. Season with pinches of coriander and sea salt. Cover and set aside.

Heat a splash of vegetable oil in a large, heavy pot on medium-high. Add onions, ginger, garlic, lemon grass, lime leaves (or zest) and the remaining curry paste and sauté for 2 to 3 minutes. Stir in coconut milk, chicken stock, mushrooms, bok choy, sugar and fish sauce and bring to a low boil. Reduce the heat to low and simmer the soup for 30 minutes.

While the soup simmers, heat a barbecue or a cast iron grill pan on medium-high. Add chicken and sear on both sides, 4 to 5 minutes per side, until nicely charred and cooked through. To test for doneness, insert a sharp knife in the thickest piece of breast. The juices should run clear. Remove from the heat, allow to cool slightly, then roughly cut into small dice.

Add chicken to the soup along with ½ of the basil and ½ of the cilantro, and simmer for another 5 minutes to allow the flavours to blend. Season to taste with more fish sauce, curry paste or fresh chilies.

Portion the soup into bowls and garnish each serving with the remaining basil and cilantro and a wedge of lime. Place sliced chilies in a small dish and make them available on the side. Serve hot.

Yummy Carrot

*a smooth carrot and coconut soup with honey, ginger,
cardamom, fresh mint and toasted coconut*

SERVES 6 TO 8

WE WANTED a memorable carrot soup on our menu, so we added coconut milk and yams to make it velvety; then ginger and citrus to give it some zing; and finally honey, spices and mint to make it fresh and unique. Looking back at the number of flavours, it seems like we might have gotten a little carried away with this recipe, but we all agreed on the result when we tasted it—yummy! And it's just as good chilled the next day. Pair this soup with our Bánh Mì sandwich (page 66).

IN A LARGE, heavy pot on high heat, bring carrots, yams, onions, celery, ginger, coconut milk, orange juice, water, honey, lime juice, turmeric, coriander and cardamom to a boil. Season to taste with sea salt and freshly ground black pepper. Reduce the heat to low and simmer the soup for 1 hour, or until the vegetables are very soft.

Using a blender or a hand blender, purée soup until very smooth. Stir in ½ of the mint. Season to taste with more sea salt and freshly ground black pepper.

Portion the soup into bowls and sprinkle each serving with the remaining mint, toasted coconut and lime zest. Serve hot, or chilled the next day.

INGREDIENTS

5 to 6 medium carrots, peeled and diced

1 medium yam, peeled and diced

1 medium white onion, diced

1 to 2 celery stalks, diced

2-inch knob of fresh ginger, peeled and chopped

2 cans (each 19 oz) coconut milk

2 cups orange juice

4 cups water

1 to 2 tbsp honey

juice and zest of 1 lime

pinch of ground turmeric

pinch of ground coriander

pinch of ground cardamom

sea salt and freshly ground black pepper

½ bunch fresh mint, chopped

unsweetened coconut flakes, toasted, for garnish

Salads & Sandwiches

....

T HE SPINACH Salad with chunks of apple and Warm Bacon
Thyme Vinaigrette and the garlicky Caesar Salad prove that
you don't mess with a good thing. These salads have been core
items on our menu since day one. Other salads have also found their
way onto our seasonal menus and into the hearts of our customers
and staff. In the recipes ahead, we hope you will find the perfect
accompaniment to go with your favourite soup or stew.

And what says comfort more than a Gooey Cheese Griller or a BBQ
Pulled Pork sandwich? Sandwiches were a late addition to our original
bowl focused menu, and on their own, or paired with a soup or salad,
they are now some of our biggest sellers and constantly win raves
from our customers. It took us some years to find the right style of
sandwich to fit the Burgoo menu. We now know they have to be hearty
and delicious, a bit challenging to eat, worthy of a knife and fork and
a little messy. Basically, if you're not using your napkin, then it's not
a Burgoo sandwich. We hope you'll discover that these menu late
bloomers are actually delicious simply on their own.

Caesar Salad

romaine lettuce with a Bistro dressing,
fresh parmesan and crunchy croutons

SERVES 6

INGREDIENTS

2 cups crusty white bread cubes

⅔ cup extra virgin olive oil
+ extra for croutons

2 large free run eggs

4 to 5 garlic cloves, chopped

2 anchovy fillets

2 tbsp capers

1 tbsp dijon mustard

2 green onions, chopped

2 to 3 sprigs fresh
parsley, chopped

juice of 2 lemons

2 tbsp sherry vinegar

1 tbsp worcestershire sauce

pinch of cayenne pepper

sea salt and freshly
ground black pepper

2 medium heads romaine
lettuce, in bite-size pieces

1 cup shredded
fresh parmesan cheese

1 lemon, in wedges, for garnish

WE HAVE kept true to the presentation of this classic salad but punched up the dressing with a bit more garlic and lemon than usual.

PREHEAT THE OVEN to 325°F. Toss bread cubes with some olive oil until well coated, then spread on a nonstick baking sheet. Toast until golden brown, 12 to 15 minutes. Remove and allow to cool.

In a blender or food processor, purée eggs, garlic, anchovies, capers, mustard, green onions, parsley, lemon juice, vinegar, Worcestershire sauce and cayenne until well combined. With the motor running, slowly add the ⅔ cup olive oil in a steady stream until the dressing has thickened. Season to taste with sea salt (if needed) and freshly ground black pepper.

In a large bowl, toss the romaine and croutons with the Caesar dressing, coating all of the leaves evenly. Portion onto 6 small plates or serve it family style in a large bowl. Sprinkle the parmesan evenly over top and garnish with lemon wedges. Serve immediately.

Grains and Greens

fresh lettuces, quinoa, pumpkin seeds, currants and cucumbers tossed with Sweet Lemon Vinaigrette

SERVES 6

THIS SALAD came together one day from ingredients we had in the kitchen at the time, but it has made enough fans to merit return visits to our menu, especially in the fall when pumpkin seeds are available.

VINAIGRETTE In a blender or using a hand blender, purée ginger, green onions, parsley, honey, spices, lemon juice, and water until smooth. With the motor running, slowly add olive oil in a steady stream until the dressing has thickened. Season to taste with sea salt and freshly ground black pepper.

SALAD In a large bowl, toss lettuces, quinoa, pumpkin seeds, currants, mint and red onions with enough vinaigrette to coat. Portion the salad onto 6 small plates or serve it family style in the large bowl. Top evenly with cucumber slices, drizzle with a little extra vinaigrette and garnish with lemon wedges. Serve immediately.

SWEET LEMON VINAIGRETTE

1-inch knob of fresh ginger, peeled and minced

3 to 4 green onions, chopped

½ bunch fresh parsley, chopped

2 tbsp honey

pinch of ground coriander

pinch of ground cardamom

pinch of ground cumin

pinch of ground turmeric

juice of 6 lemons

3 to 4 tbsp water

⅔ cup extra virgin olive oil

sea salt and freshly ground black pepper

GRAINS AND GREENS SALAD

6 handfuls wild green lettuces (any medley will do), washed and dried

1 cup cooked quinoa, room temperature

½ cup unsalted pumpkin seeds, toasted

½ cup dried unsweetened currants

½ bunch fresh mint leaves, roughly torn

½ medium red onion, sliced very thinly

Sweet Lemon Vinaigrette

1 long english cucumber, sliced thinly

1 lemon, in wedges, for garnish

The Spinach Salad

fresh spinach, apples, red onions, bacon and feta,
with a Warm Bacon Thyme Vinaigrette

SERVES 6

WARM BACON THYME VINAIGRETTE

6 to 8 strips bacon, thinly sliced widthwise

½ medium red onion, chopped

½ bunch fresh parsley, chopped

2 sprigs fresh thyme, leaves only, chopped

1 heaping tbsp brown sugar

¼ cup apple cider vinegar

splash of apple juice

sea salt and freshly ground black pepper

⅔ cup vegetable oil

SPINACH SALAD

6 handfuls fresh baby spinach leaves, washed and dried

3 apples, quartered, cored and cut in bite-size pieces

½ medium red onion, thinly sliced

Warm Bacon Thyme Vinaigrette

1 cup crumbled feta cheese

reserved cooked bacon

ONE OF the mainstays on our menu from the beginning, this salad is a celebration of bacon, so don't be put off by the extra bit of bacon fat in the dressing—it adds to the flavour. To balance the saltiness, use gala, mcintosh, fuji or any other crisp red apple that's not too sweet.

VINAIGRETTE In a small sauté pan on medium-high heat, cook bacon until most of the fat has rendered out, 4 to 5 minutes. The bacon is ready when the fat begins to foam and the meat becomes crisp, like bacon bits. Immediately remove from the heat. Transfer bacon to a paper towel lined plate to cool. Pour off the fat from the pan, reserving it for the vinaigrette. Set the meat and the fat aside. Reserve the sauté pan.

In a blender or using a hand blender, finely purée chopped red onions, parsley, thyme, bacon fat, brown sugar, vinegar and apple juice. Season to taste with sea salt and freshly ground black pepper. With the motor running, slowly add vegetable oil in a steady stream until the dressing has thickened. Transfer to the sauté pan and keep warm on low heat.

SALAD In a large bowl, toss spinach, apples and sliced red onions with enough vinaigrette to coat, then either portion onto 6 small plates or serve family style in the large bowl. Sprinkle feta and bacon lardons evenly overtop, and drizzle with a little extra vinaigrette. Serve immediately.

Springtime Crunch

crunchy slaw with jicama, fennel and daikon tossed in
Citrus Vinaigrette and sprinkled with sesame seeds

SERVES 6

CITRUS VINAIGRETTE

½ medium red onion, chopped

1-inch knob of fresh ginger,
peeled and minced

½ bunch fresh basil, chopped

½ bunch fresh mint, chopped

juice of 1 orange

juice of 2 limes

juice of 2 lemons

1 tbsp honey

pinch of ground star anise

a few drops of sesame oil

⅔ cup extra virgin olive oil

sea salt and freshly
ground black pepper

SPRINGTIME SLAW

1 medium head napa
cabbage, finely sliced

2 medium fennel
bulbs, finely sliced

1 medium jicama, peeled
and finely julienned

1 small daikon, peeled
and finely julienned

Citrus Vinaigrette

½ bunch fresh basil, finely sliced

½ bunch fresh mint, finely sliced

1 small handful toasted
sesame seeds and 1 lime,
in wedges, for garnish

THIS FUN, light salad appeared on the menu a few years ago and was equally enjoyed by staff and customers. It's perfect for spring—hence the name! The vinaigrette goes nicely on leafy lettuces as well as crunchy vegetables. The ground star anise adds a unique licorice flavour to the dressing, but substitute ground fennel seeds if you can't find it.

VINAIGRETTE In a blender or using a hand blender, purée red onions, ginger, chopped fresh basil and mint, citrus juices, honey and star anise until well combined. With the motor running, slowly add sesame and olive oils in a steady stream until the dressing has thickened. Season to taste with sea salt and freshly ground black pepper.

SLAW In a large bowl, toss cabbage, fennel, jicama and daikon with enough vinaigrette to coat and the finely sliced basil and mint. Allow to marinate for 10 minutes, then toss again. Portion onto 6 small plates or serve family style in the large bowl. Drizzle with a little extra vinaigrette, garnish with sesame seeds and lime wedges and serve immediately.

Summer Greens

*mixed greens with maple smoked wild salmon, red onions,
cucumbers and fried capers with Blackberry Vinaigrette*

SERVES 6

THIS DELICIOUS salad captures the flavours and the rhythms of a Pacific Coast summer, from the wild salmon whose runs up local rivers start off the season to the blackberries that abound near the end. The fried capers are the perfect little crunchy, salty complement. In fact, if you substitute the words "summer greens" for "Summer Breeze" in Seals and Crofts' beautiful ballad, you'll find yourself singing along.

Smoked salmon comes in many variations. For this salad we use Indian candy, a maple smoked version that comes in nuggets and that we flake apart directly into the salad.

VINAIGRETTE In a blender or using a hand blender, purée blackberries, ginger, tarragon, green onions, maple syrup and vinegar. With the motor running, slowly add olive oil in a steady stream until the dressing has thickened. Season to taste with sea salt and freshly ground black pepper.

GREENS In a small, deep-sided pot, heat vegetable oil on medium-high until it reaches 350°F (test the temperature with a deep-fry thermometer). Using a slotted spoon, carefully add capers to the oil and fry for 1 to 2 minutes or until golden brown and crisp. Transfer capers to a paper towel lined plate to drain.

In a large bowl, toss lettuces, salmon and red onions with enough vinaigrette to coat. Portion onto 6 small plates or serve family style in the large bowl. Top evenly with cucumber slices and the blackberries, drizzle with a little extra vinaigrette, then garnish with fried capers and lemon wedges. Serve immediately, while you sing.

BLACKBERRY VINAIGRETTE

1 handful fresh ripe blackberries

1-inch knob of fresh ginger, peeled and minced

½ bunch fresh tarragon, chopped

3 to 4 green onions, chopped

1 tbsp pure maple syrup

¼ cup balsamic vinegar

⅔ cup extra virgin olive oil

sea salt and freshly ground black pepper

SUMMER GREENS

1 cup vegetable oil

½ cup capers, drained, rinsed and squeezed of excess liquid

6 large handfuls wild green lettuces (any medley will do), washed and dried

2 cups flaked smoked salmon

½ medium red onion, sliced thinly

Blackberry Vinaigrette

1 long english cucumber, sliced thinly

2 handfuls fresh ripe blackberries

1 lemon, in wedges, for garnish

Winter Greens

....

fresh lettuces tossed with pears, goat cheese and
candied spiced pecans and our Cookhouse Vinaigrette

SERVES 6

THIS TRIED and true combination of greens, nuts, cheese and fruit is perfect for the winter holiday season. The spiced pecans are delicious as a snack on their own or as an addition or a garnish for any party platter. Walnut halves also work well with this recipe. The Cookhouse Vinaigrette is our house dressing and goes with almost any combination of greens and vegetables.

COOKHOUSE VINAIGRETTE In a blender or using a hand blender, purée red onions, garlic, molasses, mustard, parsley, thyme, vinegar and orange juice until well combined. With the motor running, slowly add olive oil in a steady stream until the dressing has thickened. Season to taste with sea salt and freshly ground black pepper.

WINTER SALAD Preheat the oven to 300°F and line a large baking tray with parchment paper or silicone. Whisk together the egg white, sugar, cayenne, paprika, and pinches of sea salt and freshly ground black pepper until well blended, then add pecans and toss to coat evenly. Spread out the pecans on the baking tray, trying to keep as few touching as you can manage (this approach makes it easier to break them apart after). Bake for 18 to 20 minutes until shiny and hardened. Remove from the oven, allow to cool and break apart any large pieces.

In a large bowl, toss lettuces, pears and red onions with enough vinaigrette to coat. Portion onto 6 small plates or serve family style in the large bowl. Garnish with pecans and drizzle with a little extra vinaigrette. Sprinkle crumbled goat cheese liberally over the salad and serve immediately.

COOKHOUSE VINAIGRETTE

½ medium red onion, chopped

2 to 3 garlic cloves, chopped

1 tbsp molasses

1 tbsp dijon mustard

½ bunch fresh parsley, chopped

2 sprigs fresh thyme, leaves only, chopped

¼ cup red wine vinegar

splash of orange juice

⅔ cup extra virgin olive oil

sea salt and freshly ground black pepper

WINTER SALAD

1 free-run egg, white only

¼ cup white sugar

pinch of cayenne pepper

pinch of paprika

sea salt and freshly ground black pepper

2 cups shelled pecan halves

6 large handfuls wild green lettuces (any medley will do), washed and dried

3 pears, quartered, cored and cut in bite-size pieces

½ medium red onion, thinly sliced

1 cup crumbled goat cheese

Bánh Mì Xa Xíu

....

a toasted baguette filled with barbecued pork, pickled daikon, carrots
and jalapeños, cucumbers, mixed greens, cilantro and House Mayo

PER SANDWICH

PICKLED VEGETABLES
....

3 to 4 medium carrots,
peeled and finely julienned

....

1 small daikon, peeled
and finely julienned

....

3 to 4 jalapeño peppers,
seeded and finely julienned

....

1 cup rice wine vinegar

....

1 tbsp white sugar

....

1 tsp sea salt

....

BARBECUED PORK
....

1 lb pork loin, cut lengthwise
in 1-inch-thick pieces

....

2 to 3 garlic cloves, minced

....

1-inch knob of fresh
ginger, peeled minced

....

¼ cup soy sauce

....

1 tbsp molasses

....

1 tbsp sriracha (hot chili sauce)

....

juice of 1 lime

....

freshly ground black pepper

....

pinch of ground
five-spice powder

....

a few drops of sesame oil

....

THE BÁNH MÌ is a popular Vietnamese sandwich made from various combinations of meats and pâtés, shredded vegetables and spicy condiments. Our version features barbecued pork (Xa Xíu). The recipes for the barbecued pork and pickled vegetables are more than you need for one sandwich, but leftovers are great in and on stir-fries or fried rice. Plan to marinate the pork and pickle the vegetables a few hours ahead of time, or overnight.

PICKLED VEGETABLES In a container or a jar just big enough to hold the vegetables, combine carrots, daikon and jalapeños. In a small pot on high heat, bring vinegar, sugar and sea salt to a boil. Remove from the heat, allow to cool slightly and carefully pour over the vegetables. Allow vegetables to cool to room temperature, then press them down until they are submerged, tightly seal the container and refrigerate for at least 1 hour.

BARBECUED PORK Place pork in a shallow container, then add garlic, ginger, soy sauce, molasses, sriracha, lime juice, a pinch of freshly ground black pepper, five-spice powder and sesame oil. Rub the mixture over the pork until well coated, then seal the container with a tight-fitting lid or plastic wrap and marinate, refrigerated, for at least 1 hour.

Preheat a barbecue or grill to medium-high. Remove pork loin from the marinade, scraping off any excess, and discard the marinade. Grill pork for 3 to 4 minutes per side, or until the thickest part of the meat springs back when touched and the juices run clear when poked with a knife. Set aside and allow to rest. Slice pork very thinly across the grain for your sandwiches.

BÁNH MÌ Preheat the oven to 350°F. Cut each baguette open lengthwise without cutting all the way through the bread and place, open faced, on a baking tray. Lightly toast baguette for 1 to 2 minutes. (You can also warm the pork slices, although it's not necessary.) Spread both sides of the cut bread with mayo. Top with cucumber and a generous mound of barbecued pork. Garnish with pickled vegetables, salad greens and cilantro, stuffing them into the baguette. Serve immediately.

BÁNH MÌ

1 crisp, light baguette,
5 inches long

House Mayo (page 70)

4 to 5 slices long
english cucumber

Barbecued Pork

Pickled Vegetables

1 handful lettuce or salad greens,
washed, dried and shredded

sprigs of fresh cilantro for garnish

BBQ Pulled Pork

....

a soft bun heaped full of shredded braised pork,
our downhome barbecue sauce and housemade coleslaw

PER SANDWICH

PULLED PORK
....

2 lbs pork butt (or shoulder)
....

1 tbsp thyme
....

sea salt and freshly
ground black pepper
....

2 medium onions, sliced
....

6 to 7 garlic cloves, chopped
....

¼ cup apple cider vinegar
....

¼ cup apple juice
....

BARBECUE SAUCE
....

2 medium onions, chopped
....

3 to 4 garlic cloves, chopped
....

2 cups ketchup
....

1 cup strongly brewed
black coffee
....

3 tbsp worcestershire sauce
....

3 tbsp apple cider vinegar
....

¼ cup brown sugar
....

2 tbsp dijon mustard
....

2 tbsp chipotle purée
....

1 tbsp chili powder
....

sea salt and freshly
ground black pepper
....

A PULLED PORK sandwich is just plain delicious comfort food: a mound of braised pork served with creamy coleslaw on a soft bun and doused with a tangy barbecue sauce. This version started as a feature sandwich one summer and soon became a mainstay on our menu year-round.

The pulled pork and barbecue sauce recipes make large portions, but they will keep refrigerated in an airtight container for at least a week, and the pulled pork can even be frozen in tightly sealed freezer bags for future use.

PULLED PORK Preheat the oven to 350°F. Cut pork into 2 flatter, manageable pieces. Place pork in a single layer in an ovenproof casserole or a roasting pan and season generously with thyme, sea salt and freshly ground black pepper. Add onions, garlic, vinegar and apple juice, then cover the pan tightly with aluminum foil. Braise for 4 hours, or until pork is fork tender and falling from the bone. Remove from the oven and carefully pour off the juices into a small bowl. Reserve the juices and allow the pork to cool slightly. When the meat is cool enough to handle, use your fingers to gently pull pork into long threads, discarding any large fatty pieces as you do. Place pulled pork in a large bowl, skim and discard fat from reserved juices, then add back some of juices to the pork to keep it moist. Mix well and set aside.

BARBECUE SAUCE In a large pot over medium-high heat, combine onions, garlic, ketchup, coffee, Worcestershire sauce, vinegar, brown sugar, mustard, chipotle purée, chili powder and a large pinch of sea salt and stir well. Bring to a slow boil, then reduce the heat to low and allow to simmer for about 1 hour, stirring occasionally. Remove from the heat and, using a hand blender, purée until smooth. Season to taste with sea salt and freshly ground black pepper. Set aside.

PORK SANDWICH In a small bowl, toss cabbage, green onions, vinegar and enough House Mayo to coat the vegetables. Set aside.

If the pork is cold, heat it up with a touch of barbecue sauce. Lightly toast the burger bun. On the bottom half of the bun, generously mound pulled pork and drizzle it with barbecue sauce. Top with a mound of coleslaw and finish with the top half of the bun. Serve immediately with more barbecue sauce for dipping.

PORK SANDWICH

½ small head green cabbage, thinly shredded

½ bunch green onions, thinly sliced

splash of apple cider vinegar

House Mayo (page 70)

1 burger bun, split in half

2 cups Pulled Pork

1 recipe Barbecue Sauce

The Burgoo Club

*a baguette layered with roasted chicken, tomatoes, cucumbers,
greens, House Mayo and Onion Marmalade*

PER SANDWICH

HERB ROASTED CHICKEN

4 boneless, skinless
chicken breasts

2 sprigs fresh thyme,
leaves only, chopped

2 sprigs fresh rosemary, stems
discarded and leaves chopped

sea salt and freshly
ground black pepper

extra virgin olive oil

ONION MARMALADE

3 to 4 medium red
onions, finely sliced

2 tbsp red wine vinegar

1 tbsp brown sugar

juice and zest of 1 orange

sea salt and freshly
ground black pepper

HOUSE MAYO

2 free-run eggs

juice of 4 lemons

1 tbsp dijon mustard

pinch of white sugar

2 cups vegetable or
extra virgin olive oil

sea salt and freshly
ground black pepper

OUR VERSION of a club sandwich has seen many changes over the years. We've put Caesar dressing and parmesan on one, guacamole and cheddar on another, sliced apples and brie on yet another. All these variations were fantastic additions to chicken and bacon, but this one seems to hit the mark in a very fresh and simple way. Please feel free to substitute a good storebought mayonnaise if you don't have the time to make your own.

The recipes for roasted chicken, Onion Marmalade and House Mayo make more than you need for one sandwich, but they are perfect additions to other sandwiches, salads and quick snacks.

CHICKEN Preheat the oven to 350°F. Rub chicken with thyme and rosemary, a little sea salt and freshly ground black pepper and olive oil. Transfer to a baking tray or a roasting pan and roast for 15 to 18 minutes. To test for doneness, insert a sharp knife in the thickest piece of breast. The juices should run clear. Remove from the oven and allow to cool.

ONION MARMALADE In a small pot on medium heat, combine onions, vinegar, brown sugar, orange juice and orange zest. Season to taste with sea salt and freshly ground black pepper. Cook, stirring occasionally, until all liquids are reduced and onions are soft, about 20 minutes. Set aside to cool.

HOUSE MAYO Place eggs, lemon juice, mustard and sugar in a blender or food processor. With the motor running, slowly add vegetable (or olive) oil in a steady stream until the mayo is thick. Season to taste with sea salt and freshly ground black pepper.

CLUB SANDWICH Preheat the oven to 350°F. Cut baguette open lengthwise without cutting all the way through the bread and place, open faced, on a baking tray. Spread both cut sides of the bread with Onion Marmalade, then arrange chicken on one side of the bread and bacon on the other. Lightly toast the baguette for 2 to 3 minutes. Remove warmed sandwich from the oven, spread mayo over the chicken and top with tomato, cucumber and lettuce. Serve immediately.

CLUB SANDWICH

1 rustic baguette, 5 inches long

Onion Marmalade

1 Herb Roasted Chicken breast, sliced thinly

3 strips cooked bacon

House Mayo

3 slices ripe garden tomato

3 slices long english cucumber

1 small handful lettuce or salad greens, washed, dried and shredded

Gooey Cheese Grillers

....

*grilled sandwiches made with melted mozzarella, gruyère,
emmenthal and cheddar and cut on an angle*

PER SERVING

IF THERE'S one way to describe our Gooey Grillers, it's pure decadence! They have been our most popular sandwich since we put them on the menu. Pair them with our Straight Up Tomato soup (page 50) for the perfect After School Special and relive your childhood.

We use a crusty baguette or Italian bread and slice it on a long angle, which works better than using sliced sandwich bread. Although we cook these sandwiches slightly nontraditionally, the result is a perfect blend of molten cheese, toasted buttery bread and crunchy edges that come together magically. They're so delicious that we serve 2 sandwiches per order.

PREHEAT THE OVEN to 400°F. In a large nonstick pan, melt butter on medium-high heat. Place all 4 pieces of bread close together in the pan. As the bread browns, liberally sprinkle mixed cheeses over all 4 pieces. Some of the cheese will naturally fall into the pan and in between the bread slices—or be sure to let this happen.

Place the pan on the middle rack in the oven and allow cheese to melt and just begin to brown at the edges, 5 to 6 minutes. (This will allow the bread to finish toasting and also fry those little bits of cheese that fell here and there.) Remove the pan from the oven. Using a lifter, carefully flip 2 slices of bread onto the other 2, cheese sides in. If the bread is stuck together with fried cheese, use the lifter or a knife to separate them. Stack the sandwiches on a plate, being sure to include the fried cheese from around and between the bread, and serve immediately, while the cheese is still hot and molten.

INGREDIENTS

....

knob of butter

....

4 slices of baguette, each cut ½ inch thick on a long bias

....

1 large handful mixed grated cheeses (we use a combination of mozzarella, emmenthal, gruyère and old cheddar)

....

Dos Diablos

. . . .

grilled sandwiches made with Queso Fuego,
mozzarella and cheddar and cut on an angle

PER SERVING

INGREDIENTS

knob of butter

4 slices of baguette, each
cut ½ inch thick on a long bias

2 heaping tbsp Queso Fuego
(page 21), chilled

1 large handful mixed grated
cheeses (we use a combination of
mozzarella and old cheddar, but
monterey jack works well too)

OUR STAFF occasionally get a little experimental with their meals, and adding Queso Fuego (page 21) to our Gooey Grillers turned these popular sandwiches into a staff favourite. To let our customers in on this wonderful secret, we decided to put these "two devils" on our menu. The positive response was overwhelming. Pair these spicy melts with our Sunset Corn and Chicken soup (page 53), and the flavours of Mexico and New Mexico will walk hand in hand.

PREHEAT THE OVEN to 400°F. In a large nonstick pan, melt butter on medium-high heat. Place all 4 pieces of bread close together in the pan. Immediately spread Queso Fuego evenly onto 2 of the pieces. Liberally sprinkle mixed cheeses over all 4 pieces, most of it on the naked bread slices. Some of the cheese will fall into the pan and in between the bread slices.

Place the pan on the middle rack in the oven and allow cheese to melt and just begin to brown at the edges, 5 to 6 minutes. (This process will allow the bread to finish toasting and also fry those little bits of cheese that fell here and there.) Remove the pan from the oven. Using a lifter, carefully flip 2 slices of bread onto the other 2, cheese sides in. If the bread is stuck together with fried cheese, use the lifter or a knife to separate them. Stack the sandwiches on a plate, being sure to include the fried cheese from around and between the bread, and serve immediately, while the cheese is still hot and molten.

The Vegiterranean

a grainy baguette loaded with roasted peppers and artichokes,
tomatoes, cucumbers, feta, hummus and greens

PER SANDWICH

WE ASSURE you that this recipe title is not spelled incorrectly. As the name suggests, this is a hearty vegetarian sandwich with Mediterranean flavours that hits all the right notes. The roasted artichoke and pepper mixture makes enough for several sandwiches. You can also toss leftovers with pasta, green salad, or pasta *and* greens for a delicious pasta salad!

PREHEAT THE OVEN to 350°F. Drain artichokes and peppers, squeezing out any excess liquid. Toss them with basil and olive oil, then season to taste with sea salt and freshly ground black pepper. Spoon vegetables onto a baking tray and roast for 10 to 12 minutes, or until golden. Remove from the oven and allow to cool. Leave the oven on.

Cut baguette lengthwise without cutting all the way through the bread and place, open faced, on a baking tray. Spread both cut sides of the bread with Hummus, top liberally with roasted artichokes and peppers and sprinkle generously with feta. Lightly toast the baguette for 2 to 3 minutes, until feta has lightly browned. Remove warmed sandwich from the oven and add tomato and cucumber. Lightly toss salad greens with vinaigrette (or lemon juice) and add to the baguette. Serve open faced.

INGREDIENTS

1 can (14 oz) artichoke quarters in water

1 can (19 oz) fire roasted red peppers

½ bunch fresh basil, chopped

extra virgin olive oil

sea salt and freshly ground black pepper

1 wholewheat or multigrain baguette, 5 to 6 inches long

Hummus (page 14)

crumbled feta cheese

3 slices ripe garden tomato

3 slices long english cucumber

1 small handful lettuce or salad greens, washed and dried

Cookhouse Vinaigrette (page 65) or juice of ½ lemon

Bistro Classics

....

ON TO OUR STEWS! Soups may be the backbone of our menu, but it's the stews that are the cornerstone of our concept. We have called them everything from Mainstays to Classics, but they remain those one-pot meals enjoyed by cultures around the world. Stews remind us of a simpler, slower time when cooking was done in a cast iron cauldron set over an open flame in a large stone hearth. These lovingly prepared homemade meals simmered all day, filling the house with delicious smells, and were then ladled out at dinnertime to an eagerly awaiting family.

We still use time-honoured cooking techniques—though we no longer have the cauldron, the open flame or the hearth!—and we know that these recipes will be well received by your friends and family. These classics may require some additional preparation, a little more patience and a bit more workspace, but make them step by step and the results will be delicious.

Beef Bourguignon

....

red wine braised beef with mushrooms,
caramelized pearl onions and carrots

SERVES 6 TO 8

INGREDIENTS

vegetable or extra virgin olive oil

3 lbs beef chuck, in 2-inch cubes

sea salt and freshly
ground black pepper

1 medium white onion, diced

4 to 5 medium carrots,
peeled and diced

5 to 6 garlic cloves, minced

¼ cup tomato paste

1 bottle (750 mL) of
your favourite red wine

3 cups good quality beef stock

2 to 3 bay leaves

3 tbsp potato starch

40 pearl onions, peeled

1 lb small button
mushrooms, left whole

3 to 4 sprigs fresh thyme,
leaves only, chopped

1 bunch fresh parsley, chopped

THE OFTEN mispronounced Beef Bourguignon is the most popular and longest standing dish on our classics menu. We simply love it, and we've worked hard to make it a Bistro favourite. We're humbled that you share our affection for it. In our take on this classic dish, we have omitted the traditional bacon or salt pork and used potato starch instead of wheat flour to thicken the sauce. These small changes make the dish accessible to more people, but, if you like bacon, feel free to add it to yours. Bourguignon goes really well with Homestyle Mashed Potatoes (page 127) or buttered noodles. And be sure to have at least one extra bottle of red wine and a fresh baguette on hand.

PREHEAT THE OVEN to 350°F. In a large, heavy bottomed casserole or Dutch oven, heat vegetable (or olive) oil on high. Season beef with sea salt and freshly ground black pepper, then sauté in batches until browned on all sides, about 10 minutes. Transfer cooked beef to a plate and set aside. (Cooking the beef in batches allows it to brown more evenly.)

To the pot, add diced onions and carrots and sauté for 3 to 4 minutes, until browned. Stir in garlic and sauté for another minute, then add tomato paste and cook for 1 to 2 minutes more.

Deglaze the pot with red wine (reserving ½ cup), then add beef stock and bay leaves. Season with sea salt and freshly ground black pepper, then bring the sauce to a low boil. In a small bowl, whisk the reserved wine with the potato starch to make a slurry, then whisk into the sauce. Return the beef to the pot, cover and place in the oven to begin cooking.

While beef is braising, heat a large splash of vegetable (or olive) oil in a large sauté pan on medium-high. Add pearl onions and sauté until browned on all sides, 6 to 8 minutes. Transfer the cooked onions to a bowl and set aside. Add another splash of oil to the pan, stir in mushrooms and sauté for 6 to 8 minutes or until browned.

Remove the beef from the oven, add the browned onions and mushrooms as well as the thyme and ½ of the parsley. Stir well and return to the oven for about 2 hours, or until beef and vegetables are tender and sauce has thickened. Check periodically to be sure the liquid has not evaporated too much, and add a little more wine or stock if necessary.

Remove stew from the oven after 2 hours and season to taste with sea salt and freshly ground black pepper, then serve family style or in individual bowls and garnish with the remaining parsley.

Butter Chicken

a savoury spiced tomato cream curry
with potatoes and spinach

SERVES 6 TO 8, WITH LEFTOVERS

ONE OF the more popular curries in India, butter chicken is very simple—just butter, chicken, spices, tomato and cream. We add potato and spinach to round out the vegetables and curry and fenugreek leaves for a fuller flavour. Do your best to find these two types of leaves in a specialty store, as they add a lovely aroma and an earthy flavour to this dish and many curries. This recipe is best served with a side of steamed basmati rice and/or warm naan.

PREHEAT THE OVEN to 400°F. Rub chicken breasts with 2 tbsp of the butter, ½ of the Garam Masala and a pinch of sea salt. Place in a large bowl, cover and allow to marinate for 10 minutes at room temperature.

While the chicken is marinating, heat the remaining butter in a large, heavy pot on medium-high. Add onions, ginger and garlic and cook until browned, about 8 minutes. Add the remaining Garam Masala, turmeric, curry and fenugreek leaves, and cook for 1 to 2 minutes to release the flavours. Add a small amount of chicken stock to deglaze the pan, then add the remainder with the crushed tomatoes, honey and potatoes. Season with sea salt to taste. Reduce the heat to a simmer and cook for 1 hour or until potatoes are tender and the sauce has thickened.

While the stew simmers, heat a large, heavy bottomed or cast iron frying or grill pan on medium-high. Sear chicken breasts on both sides, 5 to 6 minutes per side, until nicely charred and juices run clear when sliced at the thickest part. (Alternatively, grill them on the barbecue.) Transfer to a large plate to cool slightly, then cut into large, bite-size dice.

After 1 hour, to the simmering sauce add diced chicken, whipping cream and spinach as well as ½ of the cilantro. Simmer gently for another 10 minutes to allow the flavours to mingle. Season to taste with sea salt or more of the other spices. Serve family style or in individual bowls, and garnish with the remaining cilantro and wedges of lime on the side.

INGREDIENTS

6 to 8 medium boneless, skinless chicken breasts

8 tbsp butter, softened

8 tbsp Garam Masala (page 130)

sea salt

1 medium white onion, minced

2-inch knob of fresh ginger, peeled and minced

4 to 5 garlic cloves, minced

1 tbsp ground turmeric

4 to 5 whole curry leaves

a large pinch of fenugreek leaves

2 cups good quality chicken stock

2 cans (each 19 oz) crushed tomatoes

honey to taste

4 to 5 medium yellow fleshed potatoes, diced

1 cup whipping cream

1 large handful chopped fresh spinach

1 bunch fresh cilantro, chopped

1 lime, in wedges, for garnish

Calypso Beef

*dark rum braised beef with vegetables, olives
and mangoes in a spicy coconut curry gravy*

SERVES 6 TO 8, WITH LEFTOVERS

INGREDIENTS

vegetable or extra virgin olive oil

3 lbs beef chuck, in 2-inch cubes

6 tbsp Jerk Spice (page 130)

3 tbsp Garam Masala (page 130)

sea salt

1 medium white onion, diced

4 to 5 celery stalks, diced

5 to 6 garlic cloves, minced

2-inch knob of fresh ginger,
peeled and minced

½ cup tomato paste

½ cup dark rum

½ cup fresh pineapple juice

1 cup good quality beef stock

2 cans (each 19 oz) coconut milk

¼ cup molasses

2 to 3 medium yams,
peeled and diced

2 cups frozen lima beans, thawed

fresh ground black pepper

2 small mangoes,
peeled and diced

1 handful pitted green
olives, whole or sliced

1 bunch fresh mint, chopped

1 lime, in wedges, for garnish

THIS DISH, inspired by the Caribbean Islands, lasted only a few months in the restaurants. Sometimes a recipe simply doesn't read very well on a menu, and we were not really surprised that the idea of beef, olives, rum, curry and mango in one dish didn't appeal to a lot of people. What was surprising was that this odd combination of ingredients became a very fondly remembered staff favourite. Serve this sweet and savoury stew over steamed rice or with warm rotis on a hot summer evening. Pair it with cold beers or mojitos, and you and your guests will become converts.

PREHEAT THE OVEN to 350°F. In a large, heavy bottomed casserole or Dutch oven, heat vegetable (or olive) oil on high. Season beef with ½ of the Jerk Spice and ½ of the Garam Masala and a pinch of sea salt, then sauté in batches until browned on all sides, about 10 minutes. Transfer cooked beef to a plate as you go and set aside. (Cooking the beef in batches allows it to brown more evenly.)

To the pot, add onions and celery and sauté for 3 to 4 minutes, until browned. Stir in garlic, ginger and the remaining Jerk Spice and Garam Masala and brown for 1 minute. Add tomato paste and cook for another couple of minutes. Deglaze the pot with rum, then stir in pineapple juice, beef stock, coconut milk, molasses and a pinch of sea salt. Place the beef back into the pot, cover and cook in the oven for 1 hour.

After an hour, remove stew from the oven, add yams and lima beans and season with more sea salt and freshly ground black pepper. Stir well, add a little more stock if too much liquid has evaporated, and return stew to the oven for another hour, or until beef and vegetables are tender and sauce has thickened.

Just before serving, add mango, olives and ½ of the mint, and season once more with sea salt and spices to taste. Serve family style or in individual bowls and garnish with the remaining mint and wedges of lime.

Hungarian Beef Goulash

*beef simmered with rutabaga and cabbage
in a paprika caraway gravy*

SERVES 6 TO 8

GOULASH IS a widely popular dish across northern and eastern Europe, and Hungary has adopted it as the country's national dish. Versions of goulash vary greatly in their ingredients and even in their consistency—some serve it as a soup, others as a thick stew. What most goulash has in common is its predominant spices: paprika, caraway and marjoram. Although this dish is often served with buttered noodles and a dollop of sour cream, we use our Potato Dumplings (page 128) either stirred into the stew or served on the side.

PREHEAT THE OVEN to 350°F. In a large, heavy bottomed casserole or Dutch oven, heat vegetable (or olive) oil on high. Season beef with ½ of the paprika, sea salt and freshly ground black pepper then sauté in batches until browned on all sides, about 10 minutes. Transfer cooked beef to a plate as you go and set aside. (Cooking the beef in batches allows it to brown more evenly.)

To the pot, add onions, cabbage and rutabaga (or turnips) and sauté for 3 to 4 minutes. Stir in garlic and cook for another minute, then add tomato paste and cook for 1 to 2 minutes more. Deglaze the pot with red wine (reserving ½ cup), then add beef stock, bay leaves, the remaining paprika, caraway, marjoram and thyme. Season to taste with sea salt and freshly ground black pepper and bring the sauce to a low boil. In a small bowl, whisk the reserved wine with the potato starch to make a slurry, then whisk into the sauce. Place the beef back into the pot, cover and cook in the oven for 2 hours. Check periodically to be sure the liquid has not evaporated too much, and add a little more stock if necessary.

Remove stew from the oven after 2 hours. If necessary, return stew to the oven for a little longer until beef and vegetables are tender and sauce has thickened. Add dumplings, ½ of the parsley and vinegar and season to taste with more sea salt and freshly ground black pepper. Serve family style or in individual bowls and garnish with the remaining parsley.

INGREDIENTS

vegetable or extra virgin olive oil

3 lbs beef chuck, in 2-inch cubes

3 to 4 tbsp paprika

sea salt and freshly ground black pepper

1 medium white onion, diced

1 medium head green cabbage, diced

3 to 4 medium rutabaga or turnips, diced

5 to 6 garlic cloves, minced

¼ cup tomato paste

1 bottle (750 mL) of your favourite red wine

3 cups good quality beef stock

2 to 3 bay leaves

1 to 2 tbsp ground caraway

pinch of marjoram

pinch of thyme

3 tbsp potato starch

Potato Dumplings (page 128)

1 bunch fresh parsley, chopped

splash of sherry vinegar or red wine vinegar

Chicken Dijonnaise

*a creamy Dijon velouté full of chicken, potatoes and
peas and served in a flaky vol-au-vent*

SERVES 6 TO 8, WITH LEFTOVERS

INGREDIENTS

3 tbsp butter

3 boneless, skinless chicken
thighs, in large pieces

sea salt and freshly
ground black pepper

1 medium white onion, diced

2 to 3 celery stalks, diced

3 to 4 garlic cloves, minced

2 lbs button mushrooms, halved

4 tbsp all-purpose flour

½ bottle (375 mL) of your
favourite dry white wine

4 cups good quality chicken stock

2 tbsp herbes de provence

2 to 3 sprigs fresh thyme,
leaves only, chopped

4 cups diced,
unpeeled new potatoes

2 cups whipping cream

6 to 8 large (or 12 to 16 medium)
vol-au-vent pastry shells

2 cups frozen green peas, thawed

4 tbsp dijon mustard

1 bunch fresh parsley, chopped

THIS DISH has always been well received by our guests,
and we love it too, but it has never become one of our more
popular stews. However, thanks to a local celebrity who has
often professed her love for this dish (and the Grains and
Greens salad—page 59), it has consistently found its way onto
our menu over the years. The tangy Dijon mustard added to
the thick, creamy sauce goes so well with chicken, and we love
the visual appeal of this stew served overflowing in a light,
flaky vol-au-vent pastry shell.

Vol-au-vent is a puff pastry shaped like a pot with a lid on
it. Its name means "flies in the wind," which refers to its light-
ness: the puff pastry could fly away in any light breeze, so we
hold it down with a hearty portion of Chicken Dijonnaise, of
course... Small or large versions can be purchased already
baked or ready to bake in many specialty stores.

Herbes de provence is a savoury, floral herb blend that
frequently stars thyme, savory, fennel, lavender, basil, and
sometimes rosemary, tarragon, sage, marjoram or oregano.
Whichever blend you find will be delicious, as all of these
herbs work very well with poultry.

IN A LARGE, heavy bottomed casserole or Dutch oven, heat
butter on medium-high. Season chicken with sea salt and
freshly ground black pepper, then sauté in batches until
browned on all sides, 10 minutes. To the chicken, add onions,
celery, garlic and mushrooms and sauté, stirring well, for
another 4 to 6 minutes until golden brown. Add flour and cook
for 1 minute, stirring well, then slowly add white wine, stirring constantly to prevent clumps and keep the sauce smooth.
Reduce the heat to a simmer and add chicken stock, herbes
de provence, thyme, potatoes and whipping cream. Season to
taste with sea salt and freshly ground black pepper and stir
well. Simmer for 1 hour until the sauce has thickened.

Preheat the oven to 325°F. Place vol-au-vents on a baking
sheet and bake or reheat according to package instructions.
Set aside and keep warm.

After 1 hour, or when potatoes are soft and stew has thickened, add green peas and mustard and stir well. Season to taste with more sea salt and freshly ground black pepper. Simmer for another 3 to 4 minutes to blend all the flavours. Remove from the heat, add ½ of the parsley and stir well. Season to taste with more sea salt, pepper or mustard. Serve family style with a basket of warm vol-au-vents or ladle the stew into and over vol-au-vents, allowing the mixture to over-flow onto the plate. Garnish with the remaining parsley and top with the lid of the pastry.

Irish Lamb Stew

························

lamb braised in Guinness with turnips,
leeks and green peas

SERVES 6 TO 8, WITH LEFTOVERS

INGREDIENTS

vegetable or extra virgin olive oil

3 lbs boneless lamb
shoulder, trimmed of fat
and cut in 2-inch cubes

sea salt and freshly
ground black pepper

1 medium white onion, diced

2 leeks, white parts only, diced

3 to 4 celery stalks, diced

3 medium turnips
or rutabaga, diced

3 to 4 garlic cloves, minced

2 tall cans (each 440 mL)
Guinness (or stout)

2 cups good quality dark
vegetable or beef stock

2 to 3 bay leaves

3 tbsp potato starch

2 to 3 sprigs fresh rosemary,
stems discarded
and leaves chopped

2 to 3 sprigs fresh thyme,
leaves only, chopped

2 cups frozen green peas, thawed

1 bunch fresh parsley, chopped

Potato Dumplings (page 128)

OUR VERSION of Irish Lamb Stew uses turnips instead of carrots and Potato Dumplings instead of potatoes, and it features green peas, leeks and fresh herbs. We may have taken a few liberties with this traditional stew, but we've stayed true to its roots by braising the lamb in rich and dark Guinness!

PREHEAT THE OVEN to 350°F. In a large, heavy bottomed casserole or Dutch oven, heat vegetable (or olive) oil on high. Season lamb with sea salt and freshly ground black pepper, then sauté in batches until browned on all sides, about 10 minutes. Transfer cooked lamb to a plate as you go and set aside. (Cooking the lamb in batches allows it to brown more evenly.)

To the pot, add onions, leeks, celery and turnips (or rutabaga) and sauté for 3 to 4 minutes, until browned. Stir in garlic and sauté until browned, about 1 minute. Deglaze the pot with Guinness (reserving ½ cup), then add vegetable (or beef) stock and bay leaves. Season to taste with sea salt and freshly ground black pepper, then bring the sauce to a low boil. In a small bowl, whisk the reserved beer with the potato starch to make a slurry, then whisk into the sauce. Add lamb, rosemary and thyme to the pot, cover and cook in the oven for 2 hours. Check periodically to be sure the liquid has not evaporated too much, and add a little more stock or water if necessary.

Remove stew from the oven after 2 hours, stir in peas, ½ of the parsley and dumplings. Season to taste with sea salt and freshly ground black pepper. If necessary, return stew to the oven for a little longer until lamb and vegetables are tender and sauce has thickened. Serve family style or in individual bowls and garnish with the remaining parsley.

Jambalaya

*a traditional New Orleans style rice dish with chicken,
prawns, sausage, tomato, okra and the holy trinity*

SERVES 6 TO 8, WITH LEFTOVERS

JAMBALAYA IS a classic Louisiana creole one-pot dish that combines vegetables, meats, seafood, smoky and spicy flavours all simmered together with rice and then generously spooned out at the table. Like most dishes inspired by the Deep South, it contains the holy trinity—onions, celery and peppers—which is the foundation of Cajun and Creole cuisine as well as the traditional spicy andouille sausage. If you can't find this smoky sausage, substitute any good smoked pork sausage.

Adding the okra with the prawns near the end of the cooking time is our personal touch with this dish. This approach gives the jambalaya some extra texture and helps thicken the sauce so that it resembles porridge rather than soup.

IN A LARGE BOWL, toss chicken thighs with ½ of the Creole Spice and set aside.

In a large, heavy bottomed casserole or Dutch oven, heat vegetable oil on high. Add chicken and sauté until browned on all sides, 3 to 4 minutes. Stir in sausage and brown for another 2 to 3 minutes, then add onions, celery, red and green peppers, garlic and the remaining Creole Spice. Cook, stirring well, for another 2 to 3 minutes until golden brown. Add chicken stock, tomatoes, bay leaves and generous pinches of sea salt and freshly ground black pepper and bring to a low boil, stirring occasionally, for about 5 minutes.

Pour in the rice, stir well and cover. Reduce the heat to the lowest setting and allow to simmer for 15 to 20 minutes until rice is cooked. Add prawns, okra, oregano, thyme and ½ of the parsley, stir gently and add a little extra stock or water if the rice seems too dry. Cover and cook for another 5 to 6 minutes until prawns are pink and cooked through. Serve family style or in individual bowls and garnish with the remaining parsley.

INGREDIENTS

6 to 8 boneless, skinless chicken thighs, in quarters

6 tbsp Creole Spice (page 131)

vegetable oil

1 to 2 links andouille sausage, in ¼-inch rounds

1 medium white onion, finely chopped

3 to 4 celery stalks, finely diced

2 medium red bell peppers, finely diced

2 medium green bell peppers, finely diced

3 to 4 garlic cloves, minced

6 cups good quality chicken stock

1 can (19 oz) diced tomatoes with juice

2 to 3 bay leaves

sea salt and freshly ground black pepper

3 cups long-grain white or brown rice

20 fresh medium prawns, peeled and deveined

6 fresh okra, thinly sliced in rounds (optional)

2 sprigs fresh oregano, leaves only

2 sprigs fresh thyme, leaves only

1 bunch fresh parsley, chopped

Jerk Chicken Pepperpot

jerk spiced chicken, peppers, chickpeas
and vegetables in a rich, slow burn spicy gravy

SERVES 6 TO 8, WITH LEFTOVERS

INGREDIENTS

6 to 8 boneless,
skinless chicken breasts

8 tbsp Jerk Spice (page 130)

sea salt

vegetable oil

1 medium white
onion, finely chopped

3 to 4 celery stalks, finely diced

3 medium red bell
peppers, finely diced

3 medium green
bell peppers, finely diced

2-inch knob of fresh ginger,
peeled and minced

4 to 5 garlic cloves, minced

1 to 2 scotch bonnet or
habanero peppers (optional)

4 cups good quality chicken stock

1 cup fresh pineapple juice

¼ cup molasses

¼ cup worcestershire sauce

¼ cup brown sugar

½ cup tomato paste

2 tbsp tamarind purée

1 can (19 oz) chickpeas,
drained and rinsed

4 cups roughly chopped callaloo
greens or spinach, kale or chard

1 bunch fresh cilantro, chopped

1 lime, in wedges, for garnish

WE OCCASIONALLY stray from authentic recipes with our dishes, and this dish is the perfect example. We love many spicy Caribbean dishes and really wanted to experience these flavours in one pot. Combined here are the heat of Jamaican Jerk Spice, a rich creole inspired gravy, and lots of chicken and vegetables in a West Indian pepperpot stew. The result is a delicious, spicy summer dish best served with brown rice and rotis.

Our biggest supporter of this recipe is Ken's dad, Ken Sr., who, on the occasions we've removed the pepperpot from our menu, has made clear his disapproval in no uncertain terms. It is purely because of his love for this dish that we've often put it back on the menu. Thanks, Ken Sr., for your honesty and commitment to your favourite dish and to our bistros.

IN A LARGE bowl, toss chicken breasts with ½ of the Jerk Spice, a pinch of sea salt and enough vegetable oil to coat. Cover and allow to marinate for 10 minutes at room temperature.

While the chicken is marinating, heat vegetable oil in a large, heavy pot on medium-high. Add onions, celery, red and green peppers and cook until golden brown, 4 to 5 minutes. Stir in ginger, garlic, scotch bonnet (or habanero) peppers and the remaining Jerk Spice and sauté for 1 to 2 more minutes. Reduce the heat to a simmer and add chicken stock, pineapple juice, molasses, Worcestershire sauce, brown sugar, tomato paste, tamarind purée, chickpeas, greens and a large pinch of sea salt. Simmer for 1 hour until the sauce has thickened.

While the stew simmers, heat a large, heavy bottomed or cast iron frying or grill pan on medium-high. Sear chicken breasts on both sides, 5 to 6 minutes per side, until nicely charred, cooked through and juices run clear when sliced at the thickest part. (Alternatively, grill them on the barbecue.) Transfer to a large plate to cool slightly, then cut into large, bite-size dice.

After 1 hour, to the simmering sauce add diced chicken and ½ of the cilantro. Simmer gently for another 10 minutes to allow the flavours to mingle. Season to taste with sea salt or more Jerk Spice. Serve family style or in individual bowls, garnish with the remaining cilantro and offer wedges of lime on the side.

Kentucky Burgoo

....

*a signature southern stew of slowly cooked lamb, beef and
smoked ham with lima beans, corn, tomatoes and okra*

SERVES 6 TO 8, WITH LEFTOVERS

OUR NAMESAKE dish is a recipe our guests love or leave.
When we set out to create this stew for our first bistro, we
ordered a few cans of Burgoo straight from Kentucky, to serve
as inspiration. When the package arrived, we eagerly cooked
up one can and tasted it . . . and we promptly put our spoons
back down. The remaining cans have become permanent
decorations. Let's just say that after researching (and tasting)
many versions of Burgoo that may have contained mutton . . .
or opossum . . . or squirrel . . . , we needed to make our own. Our
Burgoo lives up to its name and has its share of loyal followers.
(Maybe one day we'll take our version to Kentucky!)

Plan to start this dish 7 to 8 hours ahead of time; you can
begin the cooking before leaving for work, then finish it when
you get home. Your kitchen will smell great! Our Burgoo is
best served with (or on top of) Homestyle Mashed Potatoes
(page 127) or warm Burgoo Biscuits (page 124).

PLACE ALL INGREDIENTS except the fresh herbs in a large
ovenproof pot or a slow cooker and stir well. Set the heat to
the lowest setting (or the oven to 200°F) and cook, covered,
for 7 hours until the meat is tender and falling apart. (You
can also cook the stew at a higher temperature, say 350°F,
for 3 hours.)

Remove the lid and stir to break the meat apart. If you
are using the pork hock, remove it, discard the cheesecloth
and separate the meat from the bones. Discard the bones,
then chop the meat and add it to the stew. If the vegetables are
not yet cooked or the stew is not yet thick, continue cooking
the stew, uncovered, for a little longer. Remove from the heat,
stir in oregano, thyme and ½ of the parsley, and season to
taste with sea salt and freshly ground black pepper. Serve
family style or in individual bowls and garnish with the
remaining parsley.

INGREDIENTS

2 lbs beef chuck, in 2-inch cubes

1 lb lamb shoulder, in 2-inch cubes

1 small smoked pork hock,
wrapped and tied in cheesecloth,
or ham, in 1-inch cubes

2 medium white onions, diced

3 to 4 celery stalks, diced

5 to 6 garlic cloves, minced

2 cans (each 19 oz)
diced tomatoes + juice

¼ cup tomato paste

2 cups good quality beef stock

2 tbsp worcestershire sauce

2 tbsp molasses

2 tbsp red wine vinegar

2 tbsp brown sugar

large pinch of chili powder

1 tbsp or more canned chipotle
peppers, puréed or chopped fine

pinch of thyme

½ small head green cabbage, diced

2 to 3 medium yellow
fleshed potatoes, diced

½ cup frozen corn

4 to 5 fresh okra,
thinly sliced in rounds

½ cup lima beans

2 to 3 sprigs fresh oregano,
leaves only, chopped

2 to 3 sprigs fresh
thyme, leaves only

1 bunch fresh parsley, chopped

sea salt and freshly
ground black pepper

Laksa Lemak

....

spicy Malaysian coconut curry noodles
with seafood, mushrooms and greens

SERVES 6 TO 8, WITH LEFTOVERS

CURRY PASTE

1 medium white onion, chopped

2-inch knob of galangal or fresh
ginger, peeled and chopped

5 to 6 garlic cloves, chopped

4 lemon grass stalks,
cores only, sliced thinly

1 to 2 fresh thai chilies,
seeded and chopped

2 tbsp shrimp paste or fish sauce

small pinch of coriander seeds

pinch of ground turmeric

LAKSA

vegetable oil

1 recipe Curry Paste

1 large handful sliced oyster or
enoki or shimeji mushrooms

½ cup fresh pineapple juice

2 cups good quality
prawn or chicken stock

2 cans (each 19 oz) coconut milk

1 lb fresh snapper,
in 2-inch diagonal slices

1 lb fresh medium prawns, peeled
and deveined (about 20 to 25)

1 lb of your favourite
fish or shellfish, cleaned and
cut in bite-size pieces

5 to 6 baby bok choy, thinly sliced

sea salt

6 to 8 portions precooked
udon or any thick noodle,
heated briefly in boiling water

MOST ASIAN countries have at least one popular and delicious noodle dish. This one is our favourite: it's from Malaysia, and it is made with a spicy and aromatic coconut broth. Our version recreates those flavours with products that are more readily available in North America.

Laksa is traditionally garnished with herbs and chilies. Serve these ingredients separately so that guests can create their own combinations and adjust the heat to their liking. You can also top the Laksa with slices of soft boiled egg, barbecued pork, chicken, pineapple and/or fried shallots. This dish is designed for a chopstick and spoon approach, and slurping is highly encouraged.

CURRY PASTE In a food processor or a blender, or in a mortar and pestle, purée or pound all paste ingredients until very finely ground.

LAKSA In a large, heavy bottomed pot, heat vegetable oil on medium-high. Add Curry Paste and cook, stirring frequently, until brown and fragrant, 5 to 6 minutes. (The oil will naturally begin to separate out from the paste.) Add mushrooms and sauté for 1 to 2 minutes. Deglaze the pot with pineapple juice, stirring well. Pour in prawn (or chicken) stock and coconut milk, bring to a boil, then reduce the heat to a simmer for 15 minutes.

Add snapper, prawns, seafood and baby bok choy and simmer for 5 to 6 minutes more until prawns are pink and firm and the seafood is cooked through. Season with sea salt to taste.

Serve noodles and coconut broth family style or in individual bowls. Layer noodles on the bottom, ladle coconut broth over the noodles, and top with seafood. Garnish with mint, basil, tofu and sprouts and serve with a wedge of lime and some chilies.

½ bunch fresh mint, finely chopped, for garnish

½ bunch fresh basil, finely chopped, for garnish

fried tofu, thinly sliced, for garnish (optional)

fresh bean or sunflower sprouts, for garnish (optional)

1 lime, in wedges, for garnish

fresh chilies or your favourite chili sauce, for garnish

Lamb Tagine

a classic Moroccan spiced lamb and vegetable dish
with sweet apricots, olives and fresh mint

SERVES 6 TO 8

INGREDIENTS

extra virgin olive oil

3 lbs boneless lamb shoulder, room temperature, trimmed of excess fat and cut in 2-inch cubes

4 tbsp Moroccan Spice (page 130)

sea salt

1 medium white onion, diced

4 to 5 medium carrots, peeled and diced

2 medium turnips or rutabaga, diced

1-inch knob of fresh ginger, peeled and minced

4 to 5 garlic cloves, minced

2 tbsp honey

¼ cup tomato paste

2 cups orange juice

4 cups good quality dark vegetable or beef stock

juice and zest of 2 lemons

3 tbsp potato starch

1 can (19 oz) chickpeas, drained and rinsed

2 small zucchini, diced

16 black olives, pitted and roughly chopped

6 dried apricots, roughly chopped

1 bunch fresh mint, chopped

freshly ground black pepper

A TAGINE (OR tajine) is the conical clay cooking vessel used to make the traditional dish that bears its name. It is meant to be simmered on the stovetop (or over hot coals), but placing the entire pot (or an equivalent casserole pot) in the oven provides an even heat that really concentrates the flavours.

Many combinations of meats and vegetables, dried fruits, olives, preserved lemons, and even nuts are possible. Our Moroccan Spice is our version of ras el hanout, a traditional spice from North Africa that can be found in specialty food stores. Experiment with your own variations of this wonderfully exotic dish. Serve with some fluffy couscous on the side.

PREHEAT THE OVEN to 350°F. In a large, heavy bottomed casserole or Dutch oven, heat olive oil on high. Season lamb with ½ of the Moroccan Spice and a little sea salt, then sauté lamb in batches until browned on all sides, about 10 minutes. Transfer cooked lamb to a plate as you go and set aside. (Cooking the lamb in batches allows it to brown more evenly.)

To the oil in the pot, add onions, carrots and turnips (or rutabaga) and sauté for 3 to 4 minutes. Stir in ginger, garlic and the remaining Moroccan Spice, and cook for another minute. Add honey and tomato paste and cook for another couple of minutes. Deglaze the pot with orange juice (reserving ½ cup), then add vegetable (or beef) stock, lemon juice, lemon zest and a little more sea salt. Bring the sauce to a low boil. In a small bowl, whisk the reserved orange juice with the potato starch to make a slurry, then whisk into the sauce. Add the lamb and chickpeas to the pot, cover and cook in the oven for 2 hours. Check periodically to be sure the liquid has not evaporated too much, and add a little stock or water if necessary.

Remove stew from the oven after 2 hours, add zucchini, olives and apricots as well as ½ of the mint and stir well. Season to taste with sea salt and freshly ground black pepper. If necessary, return stew to the oven until lamb and vegetables are tender and sauce has thickened. Serve family style or in individual bowls and garnish with the remaining mint.

Macaroni & Cheese

a Bistro favourite, loaded with
aged white cheddar and baked until golden

SERVES 6 TO 8

Thıs dısh is loved by both adults and children alike, and our guests tell us that their kids order it on their own and keep asking to come back for more. We like to keep our macaroni 'n' cheese fairly simple and cheesy so that it provides for that most basic comfort craving, but once you have this basic recipe down, you've opened the door to a whole myriad of possibilities. In this version, the flavour comes mainly from the sharpness of the extra old cheddar, so find and use the good stuff! A 5 year old is great; a 10 year old is awesome.

You can also use your imagination and experiment with additions to our Macaroni & Cheese, from sautéed mushrooms to roasted tomatoes to grilled or braised meats. See our Macaroni & More recipe (page 100) for our take.

PREHEAT THE OVEN to 400°F. Have ready a large ovenproof casserole dish or 6 to 8 individual baking dishes. Set a large pot of salted water on high heat.

Melt butter in a large saucepan on medium heat. Add onions and cook until translucent, 3 to 4 minutes. Stir in flour to make a smooth paste (called a roux). Slowly add milk, stirring constantly to prevent clumps and to keep the sauce smooth. Blend in whipping cream and nutmeg and season with sea salt and freshly ground black pepper. Cook, stirring occasionally, until this bechamel mixture thickens, 6 to 8 minutes.

While the sauce is thickening, add macaroni to the boiling water and cook according to package directions until al dente. Drain pasta and return it to the empty pot. Set aside.

Combine the cheddar and mozzarella cheeses. In the pasta cooking pot, toss pasta with ½ of the mixed cheeses. Holding a medium mesh strainer over the pot, pour the bechamel sauce through the strainer directly onto the pasta. Discard the onions. Stir well to combine pasta and sauce and transfer the cheesy noodles to the casserole dish or baking dishes, filling them generously. Top with the remaining blended cheeses and bake for 15 or 16 minutes, until the cheese is bubbly and brown on top. Serve immediately.

INGREDIENTS

4 tbsp butter

1 medium white onion, chopped

6 tbsp all-purpose flour

3 cups whole milk

2 cups whipping cream

pinch of ground nutmeg

sea salt and freshly
ground black pepper

4 to 5 cups (500 g)
dry elbow macaroni

3 cups grated extra old
white cheddar cheese

1 cup grated mozzarella cheese

Macaroni & More

....

*our original Macaroni & Cheese enhanced with bacon,
onions and thyme and baked with seasoned bread crumbs*

SERVES 6 TO 8

"MORE" MIX

6 to 8 strips bacon, in small dice

1 medium white onion, chopped

2 to 3 sprigs fresh
thyme, leaves only

½ bunch fresh parsley, chopped

2 cups thawed frozen
or fresh green peas

MACARONI & CHEESE

4 tbsp butter

1 medium white onion, chopped

6 tbsp all-purpose flour

3 cups whole milk

2 cups whipping cream

pinch of ground nutmeg

sea salt and freshly
ground black pepper

4 to 5 cups (500 g)
dry elbow macaroni

1½ cups grated extra old
white cheddar cheese

½ cup grated mozzarella cheese

1 recipe "More" Mix

2 cups panko bread crumbs or
shredded dry white bread

2 garlic cloves, minced

½ bunch fresh parsley, chopped

reserved bacon fat

START WITH our Macaroni & Cheese (page 99) and make this fine variation, which has earned its own place beside the original on our menu. This "more" version is made with fried onions, savoury bacon, soft green peas and a hint of fresh thyme and parsley. It's a nice mix of ingredients that complement each other and taste even better baked into a mac 'n' cheese! Halve the cheese in the original recipe to make way for the yummy bread crumb crust.

"MORE" MIX In a large sauté pan on medium-high heat, fry bacon until crisp, 5 to 6 minutes. Remove bacon with a slotted spoon and set aside. Add onions to the bacon fat and fry until browned, 5 to 6 minutes. Remove from the heat, and drain and reserve the fat. To the onions, add bacon, thyme, parsley and peas and stir to combine. Set aside.

MACARONI 'N' CHEESE Preheat the oven to 400°F. Have ready a large, ovenproof casserole dish or 6 to 8 individual baking dishes. Set a large pot of salted water on high heat.

Melt butter in a large saucepan on medium heat. Add onions and cook until translucent, 3 to 4 minutes. Stir in flour to make a smooth paste (called a roux). Slowly add milk, stirring constantly to prevent clumps and keep the sauce smooth. Blend in whipping cream and nutmeg and season with sea salt and freshly ground black pepper. Cook, stirring occasionally, until this bechamel mixture thickens, 6 to 8 minutes.

While the sauce is thickening, add macaroni to the boiling water and cook according to package directions until al dente. Drain pasta and return it to the empty pot. Set aside.

Combine the cheddar and mozzarella cheeses. In the pasta cooking pot, toss pasta with ½ of the mixed cheeses and the "More" Mix. Holding a medium mesh strainer over the pot, pour the bechamel sauce through the strainer directly onto the pasta. Discard the onions. Stir well to combine pasta and sauce and transfer the cheesy noodles to the casserole dish or baking dishes, filling them generously.

In a small bowl, toss bread crumbs (or shredded bread), garlic and the parsley with bacon fat to coat lightly, then sprinkle the topping evenly over the macaroni. Bake for 15 or 16 minutes, until the topping is golden on top. Serve immediately.

Mushroom Stroganoff

*a feast of wild mushrooms served in a savoury
sour cream sauce and topped with gherkins*

SERVES 6 TO 8, WITH LEFTOVERS

INGREDIENTS

2 lbs wild mushrooms

2 lbs button mushrooms

2 to 3 sprigs fresh thyme,
leaves only, chopped

sea salt and freshly
ground black pepper

extra virgin olive oil

1 medium white onion, chopped

2 to 3 celery stalks, chopped

3 to 4 garlic cloves, chopped

2 tsp paprika

4 cups good quality mushroom
stock or dark vegetable broth

1 cup whipping cream

½ cup sour cream

1 tbsp dijon mustard

½ bunch fresh parsley, chopped

12 to 16 pickled gherkins, sliced

WHO DOESN'T love mushrooms? This is the dish to make when it's mushroom-picking season and you want to celebrate the harvest with friends and family. Use any combination of wild mushrooms. Traditionally, stroganoff is served over potato straws, but buttered egg noodles and rice pilaf are also common. Steamed green beans are a great addition as well.

PREHEAT THE OVEN to 400°F. Clean and trim stems from wild mushrooms. Set stems aside and cut mushrooms into large chunks. Clean and trim stems from the button mushrooms and combine these stems with those from the wild mushrooms. Take out a handful of the largest mushrooms and combine them with the stems. Leave the smaller ones whole and combine them with the wild mushrooms for roasting. Roughly chop the large button mushrooms and all the stems, and set this mixture aside.

In a large bowl, toss the wild mushrooms and whole button mushrooms with thyme, pinches of sea salt and freshly ground black pepper and enough olive oil to coat. Arrange in a single layer on a large baking sheet. Roast the mushrooms until golden, soft and slightly dried out, 20 to 25 minutes.

While mushrooms are roasting, heat a splash of olive oil in a large, heavy bottomed pot on medium-high. Stir in onions, celery and garlic and sauté until browned, 7 to 8 minutes. Add the chopped mushrooms and stems, season with paprika and pinches of sea salt and freshly ground black pepper, and brown for another 7 to 8 minutes. Pour in stock and whipping cream and bring to a low boil, 8 to 10 minutes. (If any juices have been released from the roasting mushrooms, add these.) Remove this mixture from the heat and, using a hand blender, purée sauce until smooth. (Alternatively, allow the mixture to cool slightly and use a blender to purée the sauce in batches.)

Return the sauce to the pot, fold in the roasted mushrooms, sour cream, mustard and ½ of the parsley. Serve family style or in individual bowls. Garnish with the remaining parsley and sliced gherkins.

Seafood Moqueca

....

a seafood stew from Brazil made with coconuts,
tomatoes, peppers, cilantro and dende oil

SERVES 6 TO 8, WITH LEFTOVERS

A SIMPLE AND delicious, fresh stew, Moqueca is a traditional recipe dating back hundreds of years. There are
many regional variations throughout Brazil, but they are all
basically fish stews made from whatever fish or shellfish was
caught fresh that day. Steamed white rice goes well with this
dish, though if you're feeling adventurous try Farofa (toasted
manioc flour) or Feijoada (beans with pork), which are both
popular side dishes in Brazil.

Dende oil is a bright red oil derived from the fruit of the
oil palm, and it lends a distinct nutty, fruity flavour to many
dishes in Brazil and West Africa. It is used both as a cooking
and a flavouring oil. Adding annato or achiote to olive oil
recreates the bright colour but not necessarily the flavour,
so seek out dende oil in your local specialty food store.

HEAT DENDE (or olive) oil in a large, heavy bottomed pot on
medium-high. Add onions, red and green peppers, garlic and
ginger and sauté until onions are translucent, 4 to 6 minutes.
Add tomato paste and stir for 1 to 2 minutes, then pour in
stock and coconut milk, season with sea salt and freshly
ground black pepper and bring to a boil. Reduce the heat to
the lowest setting and simmer for 30 minutes.

Add snapper, prawns, seafood, tomatoes and palm hearts
and simmer for another 6 to 8 minutes until seafood is
cooked through. Stir in ½ of the cilantro and season to taste
with sea salt and freshly ground black pepper. Serve family
style or in individual bowls and garnish with the remaining
cilantro and lime wedges.

INGREDIENTS

dende or extra virgin olive oil

2 to 3 medium
white onions, sliced

3 medium red bell peppers, sliced

3 medium green
bell peppers, sliced

5 to 6 garlic cloves, sliced

2-inch knob of fresh ginger,
peeled and thinly sliced

¼ cup tomato paste

4 cups good quality
prawn, fish or chicken stock

1 can (19 oz) coconut milk

sea salt and freshly
ground black pepper

1 lb fresh snapper,
in 2-inch diagonal slices

1 lb fresh medium prawns, peeled
and deveined (about 20 to 25)

1 lb of your favourite fish or
shellfish, cleaned and cut
in bite-size pieces

3 to 4 fresh ripe garden
tomatoes, seeded and diced

1 can (14 oz) hearts of palm,
drained and cut in small rounds

1 bunch fresh cilantro, chopped

1 lime, in wedges, for garnish

Ratatouille Provençale

oven roasted vegetables in a savoury tomato and garlic sauce,
baked with bread crumbs and goat cheese

SERVES 6 TO 8, WITH LEFTOVERS

RATATOUILLE

extra virgin olive oil

2 medium red onions, diced

10 to 12 garlic cloves, thinly sliced

1 bottle (750 mL) of your favourite dry white wine

¼ cup tomato paste

2 cans (each 19 oz) diced tomatoes with juice or 6 to 8 ripe garden tomatoes

sea salt and freshly ground black pepper

2 large or 4 small eggplants, diced

2 large or 4 small zucchini, diced

6 to 8 medium red or yellow bell peppers, diced

½ bunch fresh oregano, chopped

1 bunch fresh basil, chopped

THIS DISH of fresh garden vegetables lightly roasted with olive oil then mixed with tomato, garlic and fresh herbs evokes summer in Provence. Although we've tried many vegetarian dishes on our menus over the years, this one has really hit home. It is now our longest-standing vegetarian classic, and it is enjoyed by carnivores, pescatarians and vegetarians alike.

We use long, slim Japanese eggplants for their creamier texture, but you can use plump, round Italian ones, if you prefer. Since we offer this stew year-round in our bistros, we opt for canned tomatoes, but by all means substitute fresh ripe tomatoes if they are calling out from your garden to be used. We top our Ratatouille with goat cheese and flavoured bread crumbs before baking to give this dish a delicious crust. If you'd like a more substantial main dish, mix in diced grilled chicken before the baking stage.

RATATOUILLE Preheat the oven to 400°F. Heat a generous splash of olive oil in a large pot on medium heat. Add onions and cook until browned, 6 to 8 minutes. Stir in garlic and sauté until golden, 2 to 3 minutes. Deglaze the pot with white wine, then add tomato paste and tomatoes, and season with generous pinches of sea salt and freshly ground black pepper. Reduce the heat to low and simmer for 30 minutes or until slightly thickened.

While the sauce simmers, combine eggplant, zucchini and bell peppers in a large bowl. Toss with olive oil to coat and season with sea salt and freshly ground black pepper. Arrange in a single layer on 1 large or 2 medium baking sheets. Roast the vegetables until golden, soft and slightly dried out, about 15 minutes. Remove from the oven and set aside. Leave the oven on.

BREAD CRUMB TOPPING In a small bowl, toss bread crumbs
(or shredded bread) with olive oil, garlic and parsley and
set aside.

FINISH RATATOUILLE When the sauce has thickened, stir in
oregano and basil, then gently mix in the roasted vegetables.
Season to taste with sea salt and more freshly ground black
pepper. Transfer the ratatouille to a large casserole dish. Top
evenly with crumbled goat cheese and bread crumbs, then
bake for 10 minutes or until the crust is a nice golden brown.
Serve family style.

BREAD CRUMB TOPPING

2 cups panko bread crumbs or
shredded dry white bread

extra virgin olive oil

1 to 2 garlic cloves, minced

½ bunch fresh parsley,
finely chopped

½ log goat cheese, crumbled

Seafood Paella

....

*a Spanish tomato saffron rice dish cooked
with chicken, chorizo, seafood and vegetables*

SERVES 6 TO 8, WITH LEFTOVERS

INGREDIENTS

6 to 8 boneless, skinless
chicken thighs, in quarters

sea salt and freshly
ground black pepper

extra virgin olive oil

2 to 3 links chorizo sausage,
in ¼-inch rounds

1 medium white onion, chopped

2 to 3 medium green
bell peppers, diced

2 to 3 medium red
bell peppers, diced

5 to 6 garlic cloves, minced

3 cups long-grain rice,
white or brown

1 tsp smoked paprika

1 tsp oregano

pinch of chili flakes

pinch of saffron threads

1 can (19 oz) diced
tomatoes with juice

6 cups good quality
chicken stock

12 to 16 fresh medium prawns,
peeled and deveined

2 cups frozen green peas, thawed

2 sprigs fresh oregano,
leaves only, chopped

1 bunch fresh parsley, chopped

1 lb fresh mussels, cleaned

1 lemon, in wedges, for garnish

ALTHOUGH IT originated in Valencia, paella can be called Spain's national dish. The fragrant flavours, bright colours and abundance of meat, vegetables and seafood make this a great presentation dish that satisfies both the eye and the appetite. Traditionally, paella is made in its namesake pan, a shallow metal two-handled pan, but you can substitute any large, wide, shallow ovenproof pan. If you have it, a large cast iron pan will work wonderfully.

To cut down the cooking time in the restaurant, we start by parcooking the rice with the saffron, then combining all the other ingredients and stirring them into the rice before finishing the dish in the oven. This recipe is more traditional, beginning by sautéing and flavouring the ingredients on the stovetop and finishing them in the oven to add a baked crunchiness to the rice and the toppings.

The secret to a good paella is to use good quality ingredients; in this dish, the flavour and aroma of the olive oil, chorizo, roast peppers and saffron really show in the final product. To add a personal artistic touch, have some fun arranging the final ingredients in pleasing patterns before baking. We serve fresh lemon wedges with the cooked paella, but if you prefer you can also add them, flesh side up, before baking, which mellows their acidity and contributes to the visual appeal of the dish.

PREHEAT THE OVEN to 350°F. In a large bowl, season chicken thighs with sea salt and freshly ground black pepper. Set aside.

Heat olive oil in a large, wide paella (or ovenproof sauté) pan on medium-high. Add chorizo and cook until the fat has rendered and flavoured the oil, 1 to 2 minutes. Stir in chicken and sauté until golden, 4 to 5 minutes. Add onions, green and red bell peppers and garlic and cook gently for another 1 to 2 minutes. Reduce the heat to medium-low, add rice, paprika, dry oregano, chili flakes and saffron and stir gently for another 1 to 2 minutes to flavour the rice. Stir in tomatoes and chicken stock, season to taste with sea salt and freshly ground

black pepper and mix until well combined. Reduce the heat to the lowest setting and simmer for 10 to 12 minutes, stirring occasionally, until rice has absorbed almost all of the liquid. The rice should be nearly cooked but slightly al dente. If the rice is too dry and hard, add a little more stock.

Turn off the heat and stir in prawns and peas, fresh oregano and ½ of the parsley. Arrange mussels evenly on top, pressing them into the rice so that they bake into it. Drizzle paella with a little olive oil and carefully transfer to the oven and bake for 10 to 12 minutes, or until the rice has absorbed the remaining liquid and has crisped a little on top. The prawns should be pink and cooked through and the mussels should have opened (discard any that have not).

Serve family style, garnished with the remaining parsley and the lemon wedges.

Turkey Dinner

*a savoury turkey stew with mushroom hazelnut
stuffing and cranberry sauce*

SERVES 6 TO 8, WITH LEFTOVERS

TURKEY STEW

¼ cup vegetable oil

3 lbs boneless, skinless
turkey thighs, room
temperature, in large pieces

sea salt and freshly
ground black pepper

1 medium white onion, chopped

3 to 4 celery stalks, chopped

2 to 3 garlic cloves, minced

1 bottle (750 mL) of your
favourite dry white wine

2 to 3 medium rutabaga, diced

2 handfuls button
mushrooms, halved

4 cups chicken or turkey stock

3 to 4 bay leaves

pinch of thyme

3 tbsp potato starch

2 cups frozen green peas, thawed

2 tbsp dijon mustard

2 to 3 sprigs fresh
rosemary, stems discarded
and leaves chopped

5 to 6 fresh sage leaves, chopped

½ bunch fresh parsley, chopped

RESTAURANT STAFF have it tough. The times when most people are enjoying holidays and long weekends are the times we work the hardest. During the first few years when we were heads down, growing our bistros, we vowed not to allow ourselves, our staff or our loyal customers to miss out on Thanksgiving turkey. In true Burgoo fashion we came up with our very own version of a turkey dinner: Turkey Stew, of course!

This stew is an easy alternative to the traditional whole roast turkey and trimmings whose preparation tends to stress out many home cooks, so we encourage you to try this recipe one day. It has now become a must-have addition to our Bistro menu every Thanksgiving, and our guests and staff alike eagerly anticipate it. A large bowl of Homestyle Mashed Potatoes (page 127) makes the perfect accompaniment.

TURKEY STEW In a large, heavy bottomed casserole or a Dutch oven, heat a large splash of vegetable oil on high. Season turkey with sea salt and freshly ground black pepper, then sauté in batches until browned on all sides, about 10 minutes. Using a slotted spoon, transfer cooked turkey to a plate as you go and set aside. (Cooking the turkey in batches allows it to brown more evenly.)

To the pot, add the remaining vegetable oil, onions and celery and sauté for 6 to 7 minutes. Stir in garlic and brown for 1 minute. Deglaze the pot with white wine (reserving ½ cup), then stir in rutabaga, mushrooms, turkey, chicken (or turkey) stock, bay leaves and thyme. Season the stew with sea salt and freshly ground black pepper and bring to a low boil. In a small bowl, whisk the reserved wine with the potato starch to make a slurry, then whisk into the sauce. Reduce the heat to low and simmer for 30 to 35 minutes, stirring occasionally, until rutabaga is soft and stew has thickened.

STUFFING While the stew simmers, preheat the oven to 400°F. Heat vegetable oil in a very large ovenproof sauté pan on medium-high. Add onions, celery and hazelnuts and sauté until golden brown, 5 to 6 minutes. Stir in garlic and cook an additional 1 to 2 minutes. Add mushrooms and sauté, stirring often, until they have released all their juices and liquid has reduced almost completely, about 10 minutes. Pour in chicken (or turkey) stock, season with rosemary, sage, sea salt and freshly ground black pepper, and simmer for 2 to 3 minutes until the flavours have blended. Remove from the heat. Using a wooden spoon, gently but thoroughly stir in the bread, allowing it to absorb all the liquid. Bake for 10 to 12 minutes until a golden crust forms on top.

CRANBERRY SAUCE While the stew simmers and the stuffing bakes, combine cranberries, Winter Spice, orange juice and sugar in a medium pot. Bring to a boil on high, then reduce the heat to medium and cook at a slow boil, stirring often, until sauce has a syrupy consistency, about 8 to 10 minutes. Most of the cranberries will have broken down, but a few will remain whole. Remove from the heat and stir well, then transfer to a serving dish and allow to cool to room temperature.

FINISH STEW To the thickened stew, add green peas, mustard, rosemary, sage and ½ of the parsley, stirring to combine. Season to taste, and simmer for an additional 3 to 4 minutes or until warmed through.

Serve the stew, Stuffing, Cranberry Sauce and mashed potatoes family style or layer spoonfuls of mashed potatoes and stuffing on individual plates, top with a heaping ladle of stew and garnish with the remaining parsley and a side of Cranberry Sauce.

STUFFING

vegetable oil

1 medium white onion, chopped

4 to 5 celery stalks, chopped

1 handful chopped hazelnuts

3 to 4 garlic cloves, minced

1 handful sliced button mushrooms

2 cups good quality chicken or turkey stock

2 to 3 sprigs fresh rosemary, stems discarded and leaves chopped

5 to 6 fresh sage leaves, chopped

sea salt and freshly ground black pepper

8 cups cubed crusty bread (any day-old bread is fine)

CRANBERRY SAUCE

3 cups whole fresh or frozen cranberries

pinch of Winter Spice (page 131)

½ cup orange juice

½ cup white sugar

burgoo

Seasonal Features

Desserts

....

FOR US, the sign of a really great dessert is that the dish comes back to the kitchen virtually licked clean. After all, what would a food for comfort menu be without a sticky sweet treat to end your meal?

We have been offering decadent desserts on our menu since day one. In keeping with our one-pot comfort theme, we serve steamed puddings, custards and other sweet dishes that can be baked quickly and served right from the dish. They are all scrumptious, but pay very close attention to three of our most popular: the Sticky Toffee Pudding, the Hot Chocolate Chili Pot and the Chocolate Banana Bread Pudding. Once you perfect these three desserts, you may never make any others.

Most baking can be a little finicky, but don't let that discourage you. Follow the instructions closely and, as in all cooking, taste along the way. Note that we use salted butter in all of our dessert recipes because we like the way a little salt complements any sweet dish, but feel free to substitute unsalted butter if you prefer.

We also think that any dessert tastes great with ice cream. Pick up a pint of good quality pure vanilla ice cream; it is the perfect accompaniment for all of the recipes to come.

Apple Crumble

sweet apples baked with oats, butter,
cinnamon and brown sugar

SERVES 6 TO 8

CRUMBLE TOPPING

¼ cup butter, cold, in small dice +
extra for greasing ramekins

1½ cups quick cooking
or large flake oats

½ cup all-purpose flour

1 cup brown sugar

pinch of cinnamon

APPLE FILLING

7 to 8 apples, unpeeled,
cored and cut in small dice

¼ cup brown sugar

pinch of cinnamon

APPLES ARE available nearly year-round, which makes this crumble a great dessert any time. When fruits and berries are in season, though, by all means take advantage of them instead. We especially like pears, peaches and strawberries. You may need to adjust the amount of sugar depending on the sweetness of the fruit, and mix in a little more cornstarch with juicier berries and fruits so that your crumble doesn't turn to soup!

Our crumble topping is very simple and straightforward, so start with this recipe and feel free to make it your own by adding some chopped nuts or shredded coconut. Make this recipe in one medium casserole dish or, as we do here, serve it in individual ramekins. Serve it with big scoops of vanilla ice cream.

CRUMBLE TOPPING Preheat the oven to 375°F. Lightly grease 6 to 8 individual ramekins.

In a food processor (or using a medium bowl and a fork), mix together oats, flour, brown sugar, ¼ cup butter and cinnamon until coarsely blended. Set aside.

APPLE FILLING In a large bowl, toss apples with brown sugar and cinnamon until evenly coated. Divide fruit evenly among the ramekins, arrange in the bottom of the dish and, using the back of a spoon, lightly press down on the fruit to distribute it evenly and fill any gaps.

FINISH CRUMBLES Sprinkle the crumble topping over the fruit, using the spoon to gently spread it evenly. Do not press down on the topping, as air pockets allow steam to escape as the fruit cooks. Place ramekins on a baking tray and bake for 30 to 35 minutes or until the topping is golden and the fruit is bubbling and tender. Remove from the oven and serve immediately.

Cherry Clafoutis

sweet black cherries baked into a moist cake batter

SERVES 6 TO 8

CLAFOUTIS IS a French dessert traditionally made with unpitted black cherries, which are said to enhance the cherry flavour and aroma, and a pancake-like batter. We've adapted it by using a richer cake-like batter and pitting the cherries so that our guests get to keep their teeth! Use this batter and cooking method with any seasonal berry, ripe peaches or plums and it's called a flaugnarde.

In the bistros, we make individual desserts in small ramekins, but the fruit studded cake looks so beautiful that we encourage you to prepare it in a wide casserole or flan dish to show it off. Serve this dessert with heaping spoonfuls of pure vanilla ice cream.

PREHEAT THE OVEN to 375°F. Lightly grease a large flan (or medium casserole) dish with butter.

Place ½ lb butter and white sugar in a large bowl. Using a whisk or a hand mixer, cream until light, airy and well combined. Beat in eggs, one at a time, mixing well after each addition.

In a small cup, lightly whisk together milk and vanilla. In a separate bowl, combine flour, baking powder and a pinch of sea salt until well mixed. Whisking constantly, slowly pour ⅓ of the flour mixture into the butter mixture, followed by ⅓ of the milk mixture. Repeat with the remaining flour and milk mixtures. Mix until batter is smooth. Set aside.

Place cherries in a medium bowl and toss lightly with ¼ cup brown sugar. Spoon the batter into your dish, spreading it evenly over the bottom of the dish. Scatter cherries on top and, using a plastic spatula, gently push them into the batter while leaving a few pieces of fruit to peek through. Sprinkle the batter with the remaining ¼ cup brown sugar. Bake for 30 to 35 minutes, or until the top is golden and a toothpick inserted into the middle of the batter comes out clean. Remove from the oven and serve immediately. Dust with icing sugar, if you like.

INGREDIENTS

½ lb butter + extra for greasing the pan, softened

1 cup white sugar

2 free-run eggs

1 cup whole milk

½ tsp vanilla extract

1½ cups all-purpose flour

1 tsp baking powder

sea salt

40 to 50 cherries, halved and pitted

½ cup brown sugar

icing sugar, for dusting (optional)

Chocolate Banana Bread Pudding

*a fluffy banana bread pudding laced
with sweet dark chocolate*

SERVES 6 TO 8

BANANA BREAD

½ cup butter + extra for
greasing the pan, softened

3 ripe bananas, peeled

1½ cups brown sugar

1 egg

¼ cup whipping cream

1½ cups all-purpose flour

2 tsp baking powder

½ tsp sea salt

BREAD PUDDINGS

butter, for greasing ramekins

1 recipe Banana Bread

2 cups dark chocolate chips,
callets or shavings

2 free-run eggs

1 cup brown sugar

2 cups whipping cream

1 cup whole milk

¼ tsp vanilla extract

THE NAME pretty much describes this dessert, so there's not much else to say other than yum! This recipe is simple to make and delicious as is, but if you want to add some chopped nuts, a few slices of banana or a handful of dried fruits—or even finish the pudding with caramel or chocolate sauce—these will only make yummy… yummier.

You can make the banana bread for this recipe ahead of time and store it, tightly wrapped in plastic wrap, at room temperature for a day or two. It's also good on its own with a cup of tea or coffee. Make individual puddings as we do at the bistros, or make one large pudding in a medium casserole dish and serve it family style. Whichever format you choose, fill the dishes for the banana bread *and* the puddings no more than 2 inches deep so that they cook evenly. Serve this dessert warm with generous scoops of vanilla ice cream.

BANANA BREAD Preheat the oven to 325°F. Lightly grease a shallow medium casserole dish with butter.

In a food processor, cream bananas, brown sugar and ½ cup butter until smooth. Add egg and whipping cream and process until smooth.

Sift flour, baking powder and sea salt into a medium bowl. Add to the banana mixture and process until just blended. Pour the batter into the casserole dish, filling it no more than 2 inches deep. Use a spatula to spread the batter evenly. Bake until bread is lightly golden and the centre springs back when pressed lightly, 18 to 20 minutes.

Turn out onto a rack and allow to cool completely. Using a sharp knife, cut the bread into 1-inch cubes.

BREAD PUDDINGS Preheat the oven to 325°F. Lightly grease 6 or 8 individual ramekins with butter and set them on a baking sheet. Divide the cubes of banana bread evenly among the dishes, alternating them with layers of chocolate chips. Set aside.

In a large bowl, whisk together eggs, brown sugar, whipping cream, milk and vanilla until sugar has dissolved. Pour this mixture into the ramekins until they are at least ¾ full. (You will have some liquid remaining.) Using a fork, lightly press the bread down and allow it to sit for 5 minutes to absorb the liquid. Evenly divide the remaining milk mixture among the ramekins and bake for 30 to 35 minutes until puddings are slightly golden and the centres spring back when lightly touched. Serve immediately so that the ice cream melts all over them!

Hot Chocolate Chili Pot

a warm bittersweet chocolate custard
with a hint of spice

SERVES 6 TO 8

INGREDIENTS

2 cups whipping cream

1 cup whole milk

pinch of cinnamon

pinch of cayenne pepper

2 cups bittersweet chocolate chips or chunks

2 whole free-run eggs

4 free-run egg yolks

½ cup white sugar

½ cup brown sugar

sea salt

A POT DE crème is simply a baked custard; a chocolate pot de crème is like a creamy hot chocolate you can eat with a spoon. And the Hot Chocolate Chili Pot is a *Mexican* hot chocolate that you can eat with a spoon. By taking a simple chocolate pot de crème recipe and adding a hint of cinnamon and some spicy chilies, we've transformed this dish into an exotic but heartwarming dessert. It may not be our most popular treat, but it has the most vocal supporters.

We use cayenne pepper to bring heat and a very slight floral aroma to this recipe, but try experimenting with ground árbol or piquín chilies, which are hotter and more complex and add a bright fruitiness to complement the chocolate. The other secret to a successful chili pot is understanding how to "temper" eggs. Adding a hot liquid to eggs directly will scramble them. Tempering is the process of slowly drizzling your hot liquid into your eggs and whisking gently until you bring both elements to about the same temperature. Be patient. Once the eggs have been tempered, you can freely mix them into the hot liquid, and the oven will finish the cooking. Although common practice is to skim off the foam that results from whisking, we like the rustic crust it forms as it bakes, and we encourage you to leave a little layer of foam on each custard.

A trick we use to test if custards are set is the "jiggle test." Remove the custard from the oven, shake it gently or tap the pot and watch closely; if the surface of the custard moves in waves, it is still liquid underneath and is not yet cooked. If it jiggles back and forth as one, with no waves, then the custard has set and is ready to serve.

PREHEAT THE OVEN to 300°F. Place 6 to 8 individual rame-kins in a large shallow baking dish. Bring a kettle of water to a boil.

In a medium pot on low heat, bring whipping cream, milk, cinnamon and cayenne to a simmer. Remove from the heat and whisk in the chocolate until melted. Set aside.

In a medium bowl, whisk eggs, egg yolks, white and brown sugars and a pinch of sea salt until sugar dissolves and the mixture is well blended. Using a ladle, slowly pour about ½ cup of the hot chocolate cream into the egg mixture, whisking constantly. Slowly add more of the cream mixture, a ½ cup at a time, until you've used about ½ of it. Once both mixtures are roughly the same temperature, add the remaining cream mixture and whisk well to combine.

Divide the custard evenly among the ramekins. Fill the baking dish with boiling water until it reaches about halfway up the ramekins. Loosely cover with a sheet of aluminum foil and bake for 30 to 40 minutes, or until custard has set. Remove from the oven and serve immediately.

Sticky Toffee Pudding

a moist spice cake made with hazelnuts
and dried fruit and topped with molten caramel

SERVES 6 TO 8

PUDDING

½ cup butter + extra
for greasing ramekins

1 cup raisins

1 cup currants

2 cups orange juice

1½ cups all-purpose flour

½ cup hazelnuts

2 tsp baking powder

½ tsp Winter Spice (page 131)

1½ cups brown sugar

2 free-run eggs

CARAMEL SAUCE

1 cup butter, softened

1½ cups whipping cream

1 cup brown sugar

¼ tsp vanilla extract

1 tsp brandy or whiskey (optional)

THIS BRITISH steamed pudding has been on our menu since the day we opened. Although this dessert is traditionally made with dates, our interpretation uses raisins and currants instead and adds hazelnuts and a little Winter Spice. The caramel sauce is easy to make and can be flavoured with a bit of whiskey or brandy if you want to add some booziness.

In the bistros, we bake this dessert in individual ramekins and, just before serving, spoon enough warm sauce over each pudding to completely fill the ramekin. At home, you could make one large pudding in a medium casserole dish and cut it into squares, or spoon the batter into 6 to 8 medium muffin tins, turn out the cooked puddings onto small plates and spoon the warm sauce on top. Whichever method you choose, a simple rule of thumb is to pour the batter about 2 inches deep, and not much more, so that it bakes evenly. Make the caramel sauce while the pudding is cooking.

Serve this dessert warm with generous scoops of fresh vanilla ice cream or, the traditional British way, topped with several lashings of cream.

PUDDING Preheat the oven to 325°F. Lightly grease 6 to 8 individual ramekins with butter.

In a medium pot on medium-high heat, boil raisins and currants in orange juice until most of the liquid has evaporated, 6 to 8 minutes. Set aside to cool slightly.

Place flour, hazelnuts, baking powder and Winter Spice in a food processor and pulse until hazelnuts are ground to a fine powder and blended into the flour. Transfer the mixture to a large bowl and set aside.

Add ½ cup butter and brown sugar to the food processor and mix until fluffy and well combined. With the motor running, add eggs, one at a time, blending until fluffy. Pour in the flour mixture and blend well. Transfer the mixture to a bowl.

Add the fruit mixture to the food processor and purée until smooth. Using a spatula, fold the fruit mixture into the batter. Divide the batter evenly among the ramekins, filling them

no more than 2 inches deep. Bake until puddings are slightly golden and the centres spring back when pressed lightly, 35 to 40 minutes.

CARAMEL SAUCE In a medium pot on medium heat, bring butter, whipping cream and brown sugar to a low rolling boil. Cook for 10 to 12 minutes, stirring occasionally, until bubbling and thickened to a heavy dark golden brown syrup. Remove from the heat and stir in the vanilla (and the brandy or whiskey).

FINISH PUDDINGS Serve the puddings warm with a generous spoonful of warm caramel over top.

Sweet Potato Cake

a versatile cake with a hint of
ginger and a warm maple bourbon sauce

SERVES 6 TO 8

SWEET POTATO CAKE

butter, for greasing ramekins

1 to 2 medium sweet
potatoes or yams

1 cup brown sugar

⅓ cup vegetable oil

2 free-run eggs

a few drops of vanilla extract

1 cup all-purpose flour

pinch of cinnamon

pinch of ground ginger

1 tsp baking powder

sea salt

MAPLE BOURBON SAUCE

½ cup brown sugar

¼ cup pure maple syrup

¼ cup whipping cream

2 tbsp butter

a few drops of vanilla extract

1 oz bourbon whiskey

SWEET POTATOES and yams often find their way into cakes and pies in the southern United States, where they lend a rich, moist texture and sweetness to any dessert. This cake has made a few appearances on our menu as a feature dessert, and it's always given our other desserts a good run for their money.

We usually bake this cake in individual ramekins, but it works equally well cooked in larger pans, so you can easily use this recipe to make layered cakes or bundt cakes. Cook the larger cakes a little bit longer and test their doneness by inserting a wooden skewer in the centre. If it comes out dry, it's done.

We use orange fleshed yams in our cake, but any yam or sweet potato will do. For the sauce, though, use pure maple syrup, as there is really no substitute. And, as always, serve this cake with a scoop or two of good quality vanilla ice cream.

SWEET POTATO CAKE Preheat the oven to 375°F. Lightly grease 6 to 8 individual ramekins with butter.

Prick sweet potatoes (or yams) with a fork and microwave on high until very tender, 6 to 8 minutes. (Alternatively, bake them, wrapped in aluminum foil, in a 350°F oven for 20 minutes until very soft.) Transfer the cooked sweet potatoes to a plate and allow them to cool to room temperature.

Using a knife or your hands, peel sweet potatoes and discard the skins. Place sweet potatoes in a bowl and mash slightly with a fork. Measure roughly 1½ cups of mashed sweet potatoes.

In a food processor, blend mashed sweet potatoes with brown sugar, slowly adding vegetable oil until you have a smooth purée. Add eggs and vanilla, pulsing until just mixed. Turn off the food processor.

In a medium bowl, sift together flour, cinnamon, ginger, baking powder and a pinch of sea salt. With the motor of the food processor running, slowly add the flour mixture to the sweet potato mixture and process until smooth. Divide the batter evenly among the ramekins, filling each of them no more than 2 inches deep. Bake until cakes are golden and the centres spring back when pressed lightly, 35 to 40 minutes. Remove from the oven and allow to cool.

MAPLE BOURBON SAUCE In a medium saucepan on medium-high heat, bring brown sugar, maple syrup, whipping cream and butter to a slow boil for 4 to 5 minutes, stirring often, until thickened and combined. Remove from the heat and stir in vanilla and bourbon. Set aside to cool slightly.

FINISH CAKES Spoon generous amounts of warm sauce over each cake. Serve immediately.

Basics

. . . .

DON'T OVERLOOK the importance of side dishes when preparing a meal for your friends, your family or even yourself—it seems the only time you hear complaints about them is when they're *not* on the table. We really like the heartiness these dishes bring to the whole meal. Whether it's our Burgoo Biscuits or our Homestyle Mashed Potatoes, we prefer a rustic approach to their preparation. With these accompaniments, it's all about flavour, not visual perfection, so if they turn out a little rougher looking than you intended, that's all the better.

Ready your pantry for surprise visitors or last-minute emergencies by keeping some spice mixes on hand. There are few moments more deflating than preparing a dish and finding out in the final steps that you're missing an important ingredient. Often this happens when you're cooking a new recipe made with an uncommon ingredient—usually an unfamiliar herb or spice. Although reading the recipe first to ensure you have everything you need on hand before beginning should help, you might be able to use one of these mixes in a pinch. These aromatic spice blends are a delight to make and a joy to use, and they bring the flavours of the world into your kitchen.

Burgoo Biscuits

....

our very own warm cheddar and parsley biscuits

YIELDS 12 TO 16 BISCUITS

INGREDIENTS

3 cups all-purpose flour +
extra for dusting

2 tbsp baking powder

sea salt

pinch of ground white pepper

½ cup butter, cold,
in cubes (¼ lb)

½ cup grated old cheddar cheese

½ bunch fresh parsley, chopped

1 cup buttermilk + 2 tbsp for glaze

WE COULDN'T serve our beloved Kentucky Burgoo (page 93) without some warm biscuits on the side, so we had to come up with a recipe. The cheddar in these biscuits has made them a perfect accompaniment to more than just Burgoo—they're great *with* any meal, *in* any dish, *on* any food or just plain, served on their own. Use a light touch when making these biscuits and work quickly so that they don't dry out and become tough.

After baking and cooling, these biscuits freeze quite nicely in resealable plastic bags. Reheat them in a warm oven to crisp the crust again.

PREHEAT THE OVEN to 400°F. Line a baking sheet with parchment paper.

In a large bowl (or a food processor), combine flour, baking powder, a pinch of sea salt and ground white pepper until well mixed. Using a fork or your hands (or the pulse setting of the food processor), work butter into the flour mixture until coarsely blended. Add cheddar and parsley and mix well, then add buttermilk and mix gently until dough just combines and is moist but not sticky. (If the dough sticks to your fingers, add a little more flour.) Do not overmix or the biscuits will be tough.

Divide the dough into 12 to 16 pieces and form into balls. (Alternatively, lightly flour a work surface and roll out the dough to a thickness of 2 inches. Use a sharp knife to cut out 12 to 16 rounds, triangles or squares.) Place biscuits on the baking sheet, brush the tops with buttermilk and bake for about 15 minutes until golden brown. Serve warm.

Homestyle Mashed Potatoes

....

creamy yukon gold potatoes with toasted garlic

SERVES 6 TO 8

WE LIKE our mashed potatoes rustic, skin on, roughly mashed with butter and cream and speckled with bits of toasted garlic. Mashed potatoes are so versatile, though, that we encourage you to make this recipe your own by adding your favourite cheese or fresh herbs during the mashing stage. We serve these mashed potatoes piled high with a well of melted butter and some chopped fresh chives or parsley.

PLACE POTATOES in a large pot, cover with water and add sea salt. Bring to a boil on high heat, then reduce the heat to a simmer and cook until fork tender, 8 to 10 minutes. Drain potatoes into a large mesh sieve and allow to air-dry for 5 minutes while you cook the garlic cream.

Return the pot to the stove on medium heat. Add ½ of the butter then the garlic and sauté until golden brown, about 2 minutes. Stir in whipping cream and bring to a simmer, then remove from the heat. Add potatoes and, using a fork or a potato masher, mash roughly with the remaining butter. Transfer to a serving dish and serve immediately.

INGREDIENTS

4 to 5 medium yukon gold or yellow fleshed potatoes, scrubbed and cut in large chunks

2 tbsp sea salt

⅓ lb butter

6 to 7 garlic cloves, minced

1 cup whipping cream

Potato Dumplings

pillowy soft potato dumplings

SERVES 4 TO 8

INGREDIENTS

2 to 3 medium yellow fleshed potatoes, peeled and halved if large

sea salt

1 free-run egg yolk

1 tsp vegetable oil

1½ to 2 cups all-purpose flour + extra for shaping dumplings

FOUND IN our Irish Lamb Stew (page 88) and Hungarian Beef Goulash (page 85), these dumplings are a fantastic addition to any stew. They're also delicious served on their own in a sauce or sautéed with butter and herbs. Essentially this is a recipe for potato gnocchi, which we find hold up nicely in a stew and take the place of plain chunks of potato.

These dumplings can be made ahead of time, rolled and cut, sprinkled liberally with flour and stored frozen in resealable bags. Use frozen dumplings straight from the freezer, cooking them in boiling water for 4 to 6 minutes.

PLACE POTATOES in a large pot, cover with water and add sea salt. Bring to a boil on high heat, then reduce the heat to a simmer and cook until fork tender, 8 to 10 minutes. Drain potatoes and arrange in a single layer on a baking sheet to cool to room temperature and air-dry a bit.

Using a box grater or a potato ricer, finely grate potatoes into a large bowl. With a fork, blend in egg yolk, then vegetable oil and finally flour until the mixture comes together and no longer sticks to the bowl.

Lightly dust a work surface with flour. Turn dough out onto the work surface and knead slightly. Divide the dough into 6 to 8 pieces. Using your hands, roll each piece into a 1-inch log, then cut each log into 1-inch "pillows." Dust these pieces liberally with flour so that they don't stick together, and place them on the baking sheet.

In a large pot, bring 8 cups water to a boil. Drop dumplings into the water, a few at a time, and cook, stirring occasionally, until they rise to the surface, 2 to 3 minutes. Using a slotted spoon, transfer dumplings to another baking sheet, keeping them separated so that they don't stick together. Add to your stew or sauté with your favourite sauce.

Spice Mixes

Making your own spice blends is a great way to personalize your dishes, so spend an afternoon making some batches and filling your home with wonderful aromas in the process. A good coffee grinder makes short work of grinding spices, although you can also use a mortar and pestle. Feel free to double or triple these batches if you wish; they scale nicely and make great gifts as well!

CURRY SPICE

Curry powder comes in many different combinations because it has travelled throughout South Asia, and each culture has adapted it to their own spices and flavour preferences. Try adding toasted coconut and or dried shrimp to this basic Indian curry to make Indonesian and Malaysian recipes.

    Heat a dry pan on medium-high. Add all the spices except the turmeric and, keeping the pan moving, lightly toast the spices until wisps of smoke start to appear. Remove from the heat immediately, add the turmeric, toss lightly and allow to cool to room temperature. Place cooled spices in a spice grinder and grind to a fine powder. Transfer to an airtight container.

CURRY SPICE

½ cup coriander seeds

¼ cup cumin seeds

2 tbsp mustard seeds

1 tbsp fenugreek seeds

1 tbsp fennel seeds

1 tbsp white peppercorns

2 tbsp ground turmeric

GARAM MASALA

2 cinnamon sticks
½ cup cumin seeds
¼ cup coriander seeds
3 to 4 dry bay leaves
2 tbsp fenugreek seeds
1 tsp whole cloves
1 tsp whole cardamom seeds
1 tbsp white peppercorns

GARAM MASALA

Garam Masala, literally translated as "hot spices," is a blend of spices that originated in northern India. Many variations, including some excellent storebought ones, are available, so feel free to try many and find your favourite.

Wrap cinnamon sticks in a clean tea towel and place on a hard countertop. Using a rolling pin or a heavy pot, crush cinnamon sticks against the countertop.

Heat a dry pan on medium-high. Unwrap the cinnamon and add it to the pan along with all the remaining spices. Keeping the pan moving, lightly toast the spices until wisps of smoke start to appear. Remove from the heat immediately and allow the spices to cool to room temperature. Place all cooled spices in a spice grinder and grind to a fine powder. Transfer to an airtight container.

MOROCCAN SPICE

8 cinnamon sticks
2 whole nutmeg
¼ cup coriander seeds
¼ cup cumin seeds
1 tsp whole cloves
1 tsp whole cardamom seeds
2 tbsp black peppercorns
4 tbsp paprika
2 tbsp ground turmeric

MOROCCAN SPICE

Ras el hanout, which combines the "best of the shop" from the spice vendors in Morocco's souks, is our inspiration for this spice mix. This blend has all the fragrance to transport you to Morocco.

Wrap cinnamon sticks and nutmeg in a clean tea towel and place on a hard countertop. Using a rolling pin or heavy pot, crush spices against the countertop.

Heat a dry pan on medium-high. Unwrap the cinnamon and nutmeg and add them to the pan along with all the remaining spices, except the turmeric. Keeping the pan moving, lightly toast the spices until wisps of smoke start to appear. Remove from the heat immediately, add turmeric, toss lightly and allow the spices to cool to room temperature.

Place all cooled spices in a spice grinder and grind to a fine powder. Transfer to an airtight container.

JERK SPICE

2 whole nutmeg
½ cup allspice berries
2 tbsp cumin seeds
2 tbsp black peppercorns
2 tbsp dry thyme leaves
¼ cup cayenne pepper

JERK SPICE

A hot Jamaican spice mix that's fantastic on barbecued meats and, of course, in our Jerk Chicken Pepperpot (page 90). Allspice and cayenne pepper are the dominant flavours in this blend, and if you want to go hotter, feel free to add scotch bonnet or habanero peppers to your dish!

Wrap nutmeg in a clean tea towel and place on a hard countertop. Using a rolling pin or heavy pot, crush nutmeg against the countertop. Place all spices in a spice grinder and grind to a fine powder. Transfer to an airtight container.

CREOLE SPICE

Creole cuisine originated in Louisiana and is a blend of Spanish, Portuguese, French, African and Caribbean influences. This blend is a staple in many creole dishes. We use cayenne pepper to provide the heat, but feel free to experiment with different dried chilies if you prefer.

Place all spices in a spice grinder and grind to a fine powder. Transfer to an airtight container.

WINTER SPICE

A blend of warm spices that evokes holiday memories, baked pies, mulled wine and roasted harvest vegetables. Pumpkin pie spice is a quick and easy substitute in a pinch.

Wrap cinnamon sticks and nutmeg in a clean tea towel and place on a hard countertop. Using a rolling pin or a heavy pot, crush spices against the countertop. Unwrap cinnamon and nutmeg and place them in a spice grinder along with allspice, cloves and cardamom. Grind to a fine powder. Transfer to an airtight container.

CREOLE SPICE

¼ cup cumin seeds

¼ cup dry thyme leaves

¼ cup dry oregano leaves

¼ cup smoked paprika

2 tbsp black peppercorns

2 tbsp cayenne pepper

WINTER SPICE

12 cinnamon sticks

4 whole nutmeg

4 tbsp allspice berries

2 tsp whole cloves

2 tsp whole cardamom seeds

Metric Conversion Chart

Weight

IMPERIAL	METRIC
1 oz	30 g
2 oz	60 g
3 oz	85 g
4 oz	115 g
5 oz	140 g
6 oz	170 g
7 oz	200 g
8 oz (½ lb)	225 g
9 oz	255 g
10 oz	285 g
11 oz	310 g
12 oz	340 g
13 oz	370 g
14 oz	400 g
15 oz	425 g
16 oz (1 lb)	455 g
2 lbs	910 g

Volume

IMPERIAL	METRIC
⅛ tsp	0.5 mL
¼ tsp	1 mL
½ tsp	2.5 mL
¾ tsp	4 mL
1 tsp	5 mL
1 Tbsp	15 mL
1½ Tbsp	23 mL
⅛ cup	30 mL
¼ cup	60 mL
⅓ cup	80 mL
½ cup	120 mL
⅔ cup	160 mL
¾ cup	180 mL
1 cup	240 mL

Oven Temperature

IMPERIAL	METRIC
150°F	65°C
250°F	120°C
275°F	135°C
300°F	150°C
325°F	160°C
350°F	180°C
375°F	190°C
400°F	200°C
425°F	220°C
450°F	230°C

Linear

IMPERIAL	METRIC
⅛ inch	3 mm
¼ inch	6 mm
½ inch	12 mm
¾ inch	2 cm
1 inch	2.5 cm
1¼ inches	3 cm
1½ inches	3.5 cm
1¾ inches	4.5 cm
2 inches	5 cm
3 inches	7.5 cm
4 inches	10 cm
5 inches	12.5 cm
6 inches	15 cm
7 inches	18 cm
12 inches	30 cm
24 inches	60 cm

Index